Human Experimentation and The Law

by
Nathan Hershey, LL.B.
and
Robert D. Miller, J.D.

Aspen Systems Corporation
Germantown, Maryland
1976

Library of Congress Catalog Card Number: 76-2179
ISBN: 0-912862-19-X

Printed in United States of America.

1 2 3 4 5

CONTENTS

INTRODUCTION

This book has been prepared for use by investigators, members of institutional review boards, and institutional administrators with responsibility for research with human subjects. The focus of the book is on institutional processes and procedures by which a proposal for research with human subjects comes under scrutiny, is assessed, and an institutional decision made. To fulfill the objective of the book, providing assistance to the three categories of persons mentioned above, forms, guidelines, and specific recommendations are included. Of course, each institution must develop its own processes and prepare its own procedures and forms based on the particular characteristics of the institution. In the development of processes and the preparation of the institution's documents, the participation of the institution's legal counsel is essential. This book is a generalized guide and serves as a point of departure for each institution to undertake to organize itself in fulfilling its responsibilities to human subjects.

Regardless of rhetoric occasionally uttered to the contrary, the authors recognize (and assume that most readers will also) that there often is conflict between the interests of subjects and investigators. Philosophically, our concern is with procedures that provide protection to subjects without unnecessarily impeding research. On a good many issues there is room for disagreement with our recommendations; comments at various places in the book reflect this. In some instances optional procedures or alternative requirements, based on approaches different from those preferred by the authors, are provided. Their presence illustrates that the authors have made some basic assumptions that underlie their recommendations, with which others may disagree, at least to some extent. For example, we believe that individuals should participate in a decision-making process affecting their lives. Thus, consent requirements are critical to the informing of subjects and are ethical imperatives, rather than recordkeeping formalities. With regard to process, we believe that formal procedures for review of any proposed activities increase the likelihood that matters on which people differ will be more fully aired.

This book is not intended to serve as a comprehensive review, or compendium, of law relating to research with human subjects or of ethical questions concerning such research. Rather, to the extent legal references are provided, they are included largely to point up the fact that statute, case law, and government regulations substantially limit the discretion that can be exercised by institutions in establishing procedures and rules governing research with human subjects without danger of unfavorable legal repercussions.

The scope of this book is limited to research with human subjects either conducted in the United States or by or on behalf of United States institutions. Other nations have differing law and different ethical and social forces affecting such research within their borders. Possibly, there are procedural requirements and legal restrictions imposed in other nations that are more stringent than those imposed by law or regulation here; but this volume does not address the issue of research with human subjects in such nations, or any country other than the United States.

Finally, the reader will note that the procedures, forms, recommendations, comments, and discussion are primarily directed toward medical research with human subjects. This reflects the emphasis given to it, in contrast with other research in which human subjects are involved. The emphasis is exemplified in part by the fact that the bulk of funded research with human subjects is medical in character. In addition, medical research is subject to the greatest amount of specific regulation because much of the regulation has been imposed through the funding mechanism. Furthermore, most discussions of research with human subjects in both popular and professional literature has been devoted to medical research. However, mention is made at many places in the book of other types of research in which the participation of human subjects is present. Most of the recommendations, particularly those concerning protocol preparation contained in Chapter 2, pertain to psychological and behavioral research with equal force, unless specific mention to the contrary appears. Furthermore, the board processes discussed in Chapter 3, the institutional administrative functions discussed in Chapter 4, and the legal principles and rules found in Chapter 5 equally suit and apply to review and oversight of nonmedical research with human subjects.

The authors acknowledge assistance in the form of comments and valuable suggestions for modification of preliminary drafts of portions of the book from Jay Katz, M.D.; Robert J. Levine, M.D.; Jean Rabinow, J.D.; and William Roach, J.D.; and the efforts of Roger Lawrence, currently a law student at St. John's University in New York City, in finding many of the statutes appearing in Chapter 5.

1

HISTORICAL DEVELOPMENTS LEADING TO INSTITUTIONAL REVIEW

Soon after the close of World War II federal funds became available in greatly increased amounts for scientific research in medicine and related fields. The dramatic growth of the National Institutes of Health (NIH), as the complex became the primary funding source for such research, demonstrated the high priority the federal government assigned to biomedical research. Although the 1970s reflect changes in the rate of increase of funds in some fields, in the absolute amount of funds in others, and in an emphasis on targeted biomedical research (such as the Cancer Conquest Program), federal grants and contracts remain the largest source of money for biomedical research.

To provide a glimpse of the magnitude of the funds devoted by the federal government to medical research, the extent of the federal funding through the NIH, and the extent of the change from the early post-World War II period, some figures are helpful. Total U.S. medical research spending in 1947 amounted to approximately $87 million, of which the federal component comprised $27 million. By

1

1952, the United States was spending $197 million on medical research, and the federal government was contributing over fifty percent of the total, approximately $103 million. From 1947 to 1952 the NIH research support rose from less than $8.5 million to almost $35 million; but as a percentage of the federal medical research support, the increase was not very large.

By 1962 the present situation of substantial federal support for medical research was already evident. Federal support increased more than 600 percent from 1952 and exceeded nonfederal medical research by more than a quarter of a billion dollars. Of the federal support, nearly two-thirds came through the NIH. In fiscal 1973, federal research support reached approximately $2.25 billion, with the NIH component (together with National Institute of Mental Health support for medical research) reaching nearly $1.5 billion.

Federally funded medical research, a "growth industry," particularly in the late 1950s and early 1960s, was essentially free from federal regulation concerning the relationship between the grantee and the investigator on the one hand and the relationship between the investigator and the human subjects on the other. As this book makes clear, federal regulations, by and large, have come to establish parameters on acceptability of biomedical research involving human subjects, once again demonstrating that regulation and control follow financial assistance.

Medical research as conducted today has little or nothing in common with the activities that early court decisions in the common law characterized as medical experimentation, yet these decisions serve as the starting point for a brief historical review of the law concerning medical research in the United States. The idea of the clinical trial in the modern sense was wholly foreign to the physician-defendant in *Slater v. Baker and Stapleton*, 95 Eng.Rep. 860 (K.B.1767), an English case that concerned the treatment of a fractured leg without the patient's consent, using a procedure that, in the light of the conditions of the patient's leg, was contrary to accepted medical practice at that time. The reported opinion, in which the Lord Chief Justice rendered his decision in favor of the patient, reads in part:

> ... When we consider the good character of Baker, we cannot well conceive why he acted in the manner he did; but many men very skilful [sic] in their profession have frequently acted out of the common way for the sake of trying experiments. Several of the witnesses proved that the callous

was formed, and that it was proper to remove plaintiff home; that he was free from pain, and able to walk with crutches. We cannot conceive what the nature of the instrument made use of is: why did Baker put it on, when he said that plaintiff had fallen into good hands, and when plaintiff only sent for him to take off the bandage? It seems as if Mr. Baker wanted to try an experiment with this new instrument.

... [I]t appears from the evidence of the surgeon that it was improper to disunite the callous without consent; this is the usage and law of surgeons: then it was ignorance and unskilfulness [*sic*] in that very particular, to do contrary to the rule of the profession, what no surgeon ought to have done; and indeed it is reasonable that a patient should be told what is about to be done to him, that he may take courage and put himself in such a situation as to enable him to undergo the operation.... For any thing that appears to the Court, this was the first experiment made with this new instrument; and if it was, it was a rash action, and he who acts rashly acts ignorantly: and although the defendants in general may be as skilful [*sic*] in their respective professions as any two gentlemen in England, yet the Court cannot help saying, that in this particular case they have acted ignorantly and unskilfully [*sic*], contrary to the known rule and usage of surgeons.

A nineteenth century New York state decision, *Carpenter v. Blake*, 60 Barb. (N.Y.) 488 (1871), also characterized an instance of malpractice as experimentation. The principle emerging from the opinion in that case, even more clearly than from *Slater v. Baker and Stapleton*, was that one who experiments with an innovative treatment is responsible for all harm that follows.

To place in perspective these court decisions and the few others that characterized various deviant medical practice as experimentation, it is appropriate to recognize that the ultimate defense in a malpractice suit logically would be to claim that the physician deviated from recognized practice because he was attempting to improve upon it by experimenting with another therapeutic approach. Medical treatment can be divided into three broad categories: therapeutic approaches within the range of accepted medical practice, those not within such practice but used as part of an investigation conducted in a manner consistent with principles governing research with human subjects, and those that are neither accepted medical practice nor part of such an investigation. The early court decisions suggest, particularly by their recognition of the need for consent, that in providing unorthodox therapy the failure to indicate to the patient that accepted medical practice is not followed puts the treatment into the third category, substantially enhancing the risk of liability for medical malpractice. Some might term it quackery.

Many changes occurred in the design of research between these early cases and World War II. Statistics, the theoretical basis for most elements of research design, did not begin developing until the late eighteenth century. Pierre Simon LaPlace, a French mathematician, suggested the application of statistics to experimentation in 1814, proposing the use of two groups of subjects, one treated and the other serving as a control. Over fifty years earlier the Irish philosopher George Berkeley had suggested a similar design in an effort to prove the curative powers of his favorite remedy, tar-water. A few great men of science conducted controlled studies in the eighteenth century, most notably James Lind's study of the effects of citrus fruits on scurvy in the 1750s and the English physician Edward Jenner's study of innoculation with cowpox as a preventive for smallpox in the 1790s. There may have been some other earlier controlled studies. However, controlled studies were not widely pursued until the twentieth century. One of the first uses of randomization in the assigning of subjects to the control group was in nutritionist Horace Fletcher's study of the effect of dietary factors on beriberi in 1907.

Tests of statistical significance entered the scene in 1900 with Karl Pearson's development of the "chi-square" test. Research involving a small number of subjects was given a theoretical foundation when "student's t-test" was introduced in 1908. This date curiously coincides with the creation of Ira Remsen's board by President Theodore Roosevelt to study the effects of boric acid and sacchrine on the human body, one of the first federal efforts in biomedical research.

Study design and statistical analysis of data became widely publicized in the 1930s with the publication of the book by British scientist Ronald A. Fisher on the design of experiments in 1935 and Sir Austin Bradford Hill's series of articles on medical statistics in *Lancet* in 1937.

The double-blind controlled study, in which neither the subjects nor the investigators know which subjects are in the control group, was first proposed in the 1940s. One of the earliest uses of that design was in England in 1949-1950 in the Medical Research Council's study of the effectiveness of antihistamines in the prevention and treatment of the common cold.

The first major effort of law to grapple with the problems of modern biomedical research was the prosecution of Karl Brandt and others by the Nuremburg Military Tribunal for the way in which medical experiments were conducted by the Nazis on persons in concentration camps. To lay the basis for the decisions by the Tribunal as to guilt of the defendants who had participated in the medical experiments, a set of basic principles embodying moral, ethical, and legal concepts for the conduct of acceptable experiments had to be introduced before the Tribunal as the standard against which the activities of the defendants would be measured. Although all war crimes trials, including the case concerning medical experiments, were considered by some to be based on legal principles not previously established under international law, there was widespread support both within the medical profession and the general community concerning the appropriateness of the principles constituting the standards in the Medical Case, both for use there and as a point of departure for establishing standards for the conduct of research with human subjects in the future. Thus the "Nuremburg Code," although subjected to considerable critical analysis and "refined" in later pronouncements of national and international organizations concerning standards for ethical research, represented a substantially more sophisticated and useful guide for evaluation of research activity than the handful of court decisions concerning the performance of individual physicians characterized as experimentation in malpractice litigation.

Federal regulation of biomedical research has come primarily from the Department of Health, Education and Welfare pursuant to its powers under the Public Health Services Act to regulate research for which it provides funds, and through the Food and Drug Administration (FDA), by establishing the standards for research the FDA will accept as evidence of the safety and efficacy of drugs. Some sources say that federal regulation of research programs began with a 1953 NIH requirement that research involving humans at its Clinical Center in Bethesda be first approved by a review committee responsible for the protection of human subjects. In 1966 the Surgeon General extended the requirement of prior review by a committee of "institutional associates" to all "extramural" research supported by USPHS research or research training grants. Prior committee review was instituted for intramural research programs of the USPHS in 1967. *The Institutional Guide to DHEW Policy on the Protection of Human Subjects* was published in 1971. Formal regulations were first published in the *Federal Register* on May 30, 1974, and became effective on July 1, 1974. There were technical amendments on March 13, 1975; and the regulations were renumbered on August 8, 1975, at the time a new part was added regulating research involving fetuses, pregnant women, and *in vitro* fertilization. This acceleration of regulatory activity probably was prompted by congressional efforts to establish a commission to protect human subjects of research, culminating in Title II of the National Research Act, which was signed into law on July 12, 1974. Title II created the National Commission for the Protection of Human Subjects of Biomedical and Behavioral Research, which has been given the responsibility to investigate, develop guidelines, and make recommendations concerning some central issues of research involving human subjects.

FDA research regulations were prompted by a specific congressional mandate, much earlier than the DHEW regulations. The 1962 amendments to the Federal Food, Drug, and Cosmetic Act added the requirement that the informed consent of all subjects of new drug experiments should be obtained. Pursuant to the statute, the FDA published a statement of policy in 1967, and in 1971 the FDA added the requirement of institutional committee review of clinical investigations of new drugs in human beings.

During the 1960s and 1970s several research projects conducted in an unacceptable manner received widespread publicity and extensive official scrutiny. Their disclosure contributed to the support for closer oversight of research, which resulted in the regulations mentioned above and in the variety of state laws and regulations presented in Chapter 5. Three of the research studies are discussed below: the Jewish Chronic Disease Hospital cancer study, the Milledgeville State Hospital drug studies, and the USPHS Tuskegee syphilis study.

JEWISH CHRONIC DISEASE HOSPITAL

The proceedings following a hypodermic injection of suspensions containing cells from cultures of human cancer tissue into twenty-two patients at Jewish Chronic Disease Hospital (JCDH) in Brooklyn were the most highly publicized event dealing with a plannned research study with human subjects in the 1960s. A lawsuit brought by a member of the hospital's board of directors resulted in a New York Court of Appeals decision, *Hyman v. Jewish Chronic Disease Hospital*, 206 N. E. 2d 338 (1965), which recognized the director's interest in access to patient records that would indicate the extent to which patients had been made subjects in the study of rejection responses to live cancer cells. The expressed concern was threefold: to protect the institution's reputation, to prevent abuses to patients, and to obtain information that would indicate the extent of possible institutional liability resulting from injections given as part of the study.

A petition to bring about the revocation of the licenses of two physicians intimately involved in the study, primarily on the grounds that effective consent of the subjects was not secured and that fraud and deceit were employed by the physicians in dealing with subjects of the study, ultimately led to the suspension of their licenses by the Board of Regents. The board stayed the execution of the suspension and placed the physicians on probation for a period of one year. One of the most telling points to emerge from the license revocation proceeding was the reason that the subjects were not informed that the injected material contained live cancer cells: the investigators wished to avoid both emotional responses from the patients and refusals of participation.

The license revocation proceeding was not devoted to failings of institutional processes to any substantial extent. However, proceeding documents indicate that the study was not presented to the research committee of JCDH and that the approval of several physicians who had direct patient care responsibilities for the subjects in the study was neither solicited nor received prior to the injections. In fact, several resident physicians on the hospital staff when presented with the project indicated that participation of JCDH patients should be rejected because of anticipated problems with securing informed consent.

Particularly noteworthy was the fact that the live cancer cell injections were given at the behest of a physician-investigator who had no connection with JCDH as part of his research endeavors as an employee of another institution, Sloan-Kettering Institute for Cancer Research. There is nothing in the proceedings to indicate that Sloan-Kettering conducted any institutional review of the research project.

MILLEDGEVILLE STATE HOSPITAL

In 1969 at the request of the governor of Georgia, the president of the Medical Association of Georgia appointed a committee to investigate charges relating to staff practices at the Milledgeville State Hospital, a large institution for patients with mental disorders. The committee also was given a mandate to develop recommendations concerning the administration and professional staffing of the institution. Part of the report was a review of an investigational drug program conducted at Milledgeville in which patients were administered investigational drugs by the assistant medical director of one of its units. Several practices in the investigational drug program were found to need change. The investigator had not obtained the opinion of the clinical psychiatrist responsible for the care of the particular patient, consent had not been obtained for the administration of investigational drugs from the patient or anyone else on behalf of the patient, and there was no explicit review or institutional approval of the program. In its recommendations the committee urged changes in consent practices, the establishment of a research committee of five staff physicians plus the superintendent to review each investigational drug program and to decide whether to permit it, the creation of the position of Director of Research at the institution, and the imposition of the requirement that, except in an emergency, investigational drugs be administered only after an affirmative finding in writing by two staff physicians, one of whom was the clinical psychiatrist responsible for the particular patient, that the specific drug is indicated for treatment of the patient's physical or mental condition.

Noteworthy is the emphasis on procedure: review of each investigational drug program by an institutional committee is recommended, and also endorsed is a requirement that the investigator's judgment as to administration of an agent be consistent with the judgment of the physician with patient care responsibility, which recognizes the separate roles of the investigator and the attending physician.

TUSKEGEE SYPHILIS STUDY

In the early 1930s a study (which was to gain considerable notoriety in the 1970s) was initiated by the USPHS. The Tuskegee study, as it came to be known, was a long-term investigation of untreated syphilis involving two groups of Negro males; one group consisted of those who had untreated syphilis, and a second group, having approximately half as many members, contained those judged free of the disease. During the study, which continued until 1973, the participants were examined periodically to follow the natural course of syphilis. No treatment of syphilis was provided, even to those in the control group; and the withholding of treatment remained part of the study even after penicillin therapy became generally available in the early 1950s. Steps were even taken to keep the subjects from obtaining treatment for syphilis from other sources. The participants did have other medical and health services provided to them. Autopsies were performed on most of the participants who died.

After the Tuskegee study came to public attention, a report prepared by an ad hoc advisory panel to the Assistant Secretary for Health in 1973 concluded, among other things, that informed consent of the participants had not been secured and that standardized evaluation procedures were not employed. Subsequent litigation on behalf of the survivors and the families of deceased subjects resulted in settlements ranging from $37,500 for survivors who had syphilis to $5,000 for the estates of deceased participants who did not contract syphilis.

That the study was ever begun is of less importance in considering the historical background leading to the development of formal institutional review procedures than is the fact that the study was continued for approximately forty years and was halted only after widespread national publicity and the recommendation to end the study by an ad hoc advisory panel. During the time the study was in progress many events occurred and many regulations and codes were promulgated that shaped and expressed the views of both investigators and the public concerning research involving human subjects without any apparent impact on the Tuskegee study, which appears to have had a momentum of its own. The Nuremburg Code contained a number of elements that the Tuskegee study continued clearly to violate, most prominently the requirement of free and informed consent of the subjects. Other pronouncements of medical organizations on the ethics of research were widely publicized without apparent effect on the Tuskegee study. The cancer cell injection incident at JCDH and the investigation that followed dramatically alerted investigators to the issue of consent. But what makes it most difficult to understand why the study was allowed to continue is that the DHEW began requiring review of some research in 1953, and in 1967 subjected all intramural (internal) research programs of the USPHS, of which the Tuskegee study was one, to committee review. However, the review requirement applied directly only to new studies. Perhaps the absence of any applicable specific requirement for periodic or continuing review accounts for the seeming contradiction between what the DHEW was seeking to achieve through regulation and the manner in which one of its longest studies was conducted during the same period.

In 1969 an ad hoc committee to review the Tuskegee study and to determine whether the study should continue was created; it met for one afternoon session. Although the committee concluded that this type of study would never be repeated, it did not suggest that it be terminated or that the consent of the subjects be obtained. Whether this committee recognized the implications of the study and its departure from the standards concerning acceptable investigations with human subjects is not clear. The standards, guidelines, and policies being formulated by the DHEW for extramural and intramural research and the publicity surrounding incidents involving questionable research practices evidently had no impact on the Tuskegee study at that time.

INSTITUTIONAL REVIEW

The preceeding events note the increasing recognition of a responsibility to conduct institutional review both prior to the commencement of research involving human subjects and during the performance of such research as an attempt to protect the rights and welfare of subjects from the potential for abuse by investigators. Although procedures, policy documents, and codes cannot in themselves guarantee the integrity of the investigator in the conduct of research, oversight through institutional processes by both professional peers and other persons aware of the rights of subjects diminishes the likelihood that ethical and legal abuses of the investigator-subject relationship will occur. Quite simply, institutional review represents recognition of the dangers of relying on the investigator to assess and protect the interests of the subject when there is a potential or actual conflict of interest between the investigator's research interests and the interests of those who would be subjects in the study. Whether formal institutional oversight procedures by their very existence unreasonably impugn the integrity of investigators may well be a question for legitimate debate. Yet, such oversight is for the purpose of bringing to bear objective assessment of proposals for research activities and their conduct. All regulation of activity conducted by humans can be taken to denote doubt that ethical and legal requirements will be met solely through the exercise of individual integrity, particularly when it involves contact with others, which has a potential for exploitation. Given the elements of the usual relationship between the investigator and the subject, it is perhaps surprising that institutional review of any rigor has been so late in coming and is (except for research supported by DHEW funds or submitted to the FDA) so far from universally mandated by law.

Institutional review requirements are not intended and should not be taken to imply any lessening of investigator responsibility to design and conduct a study consistent with ethical and legal principles. Rather they should be recognized as imposing a process in addition to the investigator's own consideration of a proposed study and of the risks that could be associated with participation in it. The approval of a study after institutional review procedures have been completed does not mean that the investigator is then insulated from personal liability for harm suffered by subjects in the study caused by negligence or malpractice. All manner of complex questions of the standard to be applied in determining whether negligence or malpractice occurred may be presented in litigation. However, an incisive institutional review process conducted by persons who understand and fulfill their responsibilities as members of the board or committee should reduce the potential risk of liability to which the investigator is exposed below that which might be anticipated when the investigator was not required to submit his proposal for such review. This is most likely with regard to liability based on failure to secure a subject's informed consent.

Recognition must also be given to the limits of institutional review procedures in safeguarding the rights and welfare of subjects. The typical institutional review board does not possess the means to determine whether the proposal as approved is adhered to by the investigator unless complaints or inquiries are brought to its attention. In large measure, the continuing oversight and periodic review depends on the information provided by the investigator to the institutional review board. The quality and completeness of the information, in turn, depend on the integrity and capability of the investigators and their willingness to abide by the ethical and legal principles of which they are assumed to be aware. Since institutional review processes do not supplant the investigator's personal responsibility in the conduct of research, it is apparent that the investigator's liability under the law remains for harm resulting from conduct that fails to meet standards applicable to the activities in which he is engaged.

2

THE INVESTIGATOR'S PRESENTATION TO THE BOARD

Increasingly, review of proposed investigations involving human subjects has been either required or voluntarily adopted. This chapter and the two that follow it are aimed at facilitating that review. The opening portion of this chapter outlines the review of a research project so the interrelationship of these chapters can be seen.

The primary responsibility for each investigation remains with the investigator. The investigator conceives the study and designs it, usually with the assistance of colleagues and consultants. This chapter can assist the investigator in avoiding some problems when designing the study. After the study is designed the investigator prepares a consent form to present to proposed subjects and a protocol describing the aspects of the study of concern to the Institutional Review Board. The investigator submits both documents for review. This chapter is organized to help the investigator prepare these documents to present all relevant information so review can take place without avoidable delay.

The review by the board of the protocol and consent form is primarily to protect the subjects by introducing objective scrutiny of the proposed research by a number of persons with a wide range of perspectives. The board review process permits societal values to be expressed and to be taken into account; this can increase public acceptance of the scientific enterprise. Review can also help in-

13

vestigators avoid inadvertently placing themselves or their subjects at unnecessary risk. Chapter 3 is designed to provide a framework and a suggested procedure for the board review, and it can be used to provide a focus for the board in developing its policies. Even if the board does not choose to adopt such a formal analysis, Chapter 3 should help to orient individual board members (especially new members) to their duties. Since the board has a responsibility to assess the acceptability of proposed investigations from many perspectives, new members often find that it takes some time to understand concerns that are outside their usual areas of activity.

The consent form often provides the only problem in review; and, fortunately, difficulties with it are often the easiest to correct. The problem arises because of confusion over the function of the consent form. It is not a release; it is not exculpatory (the DHEW prohibits exculpatory clauses in consent forms). It is evidence of consent and evidence of the disclosure of essential information to the subject necessary to make that consent an informed consent. It also can be used as the vehicle for the disclosure. The consent form can be used to attempt to increase the probability of truly voluntary consent by correcting mistaken beliefs concerning the consequences of consent that might improperly influence the decision. This chapter describes how to prepare and to use a consent form to satisfy all these functions.

Institutional review should be an interactional process between the board and the investigator, striving to find a way that the proposed study can be performed in a manner consistent with public policy and the rights and welfare of the subjects, without destroying the scientific worth of the study. This should not be done by ignoring problems but by fashioning approaches that remove the problems or reduce them to acceptable levels. This can best be accomplished when the problems are clearly understood. Chapters 2 and 3 should help focus consideration on the critical issues. It is not always possible to find an acceptable manner to conduct a particular study. But if the issues are made clear and serious, interactional efforts take place, rejections of proposals more likely will be based on recognized principles rather than personal opinions.

Board approval ordinarily must be ratified by institutional officials before the study can be conducted. This is a requirement when DHEW support is involved. The institution has an opportunity to override board approval; however, the institution cannot override board disapproval. Thus, the institution and the board jointly have the power to establish broad institutional policies concerning research. However, the allocation of responsibility for establishing the specific policies of the institution will depend on the nature and organizational structure of the institution; the administration may defer on proposing policy and similar matters where board expertise is crucial.

Once the research proposal is approved, the conduct of the study is the responsibility of the investigator. The investigator must conduct the study in the manner that was approved, subject to board oversight. Modifications must be approved by the board before they are introduced into the study. Unexpected results detrimental to the subjects must be reported to the board so it can review any action taken by the investigator. This requirement is designed to protect the subjects; the board can take additional action where it finds such action warranted.

If the study extends beyond the time approved by the board, the investigator must resubmit the protocol and the consent form for review and reapproval. This should not be a perfunctory review. The results of the first part of the study might indicate needed changes in either the study design or the consent form. Changes in the law or public attitudes also might have occurred, and these could call for changes as well.

GUIDELINES FOR PROTOCOL PREPARATION

The Institutional Review Board must have information about a proposed investigation before it can take any action or reach any decision with regard to it. The protocol is the instrument by which the investigator presents that information to the board. However, the investigator needs an outline of what the board needs and expects so the protocol can be complete and focused on the information relevant to the board's concerns. The board has the responsibility to provide this guidance, both to assist the investigator and to facilitate the performance of its functions. Preparation of the protocol in line with the board's format could focus more attention on some of the effects of the study on the subjects, perhaps leading to modifications of the study design for their protection and comfort.

The investigator has the responsibility to prepare a form for subject consent. The board has the responsibility to assure that the consent form discloses all necessary information in language that the subject reasonably can be expected to understand and that clearly indicates to the subject that there is a choice to be made. This has frequently required the board to spend a great deal of time revising consent forms submitted by investigators.   By providing investigators with a guide for the initial preparation of consent forms, some (but not all) of this revising activity by the board can be eliminated.

We suggest that a set of guidelines similar to those that follow be prepared at your institution and be made available to investigators. The comments following some of the paragraphs are not intended to be part of the guidelines. They are designed to aid in the modification of the guidelines to fit the organization and philosophy of the individual institution.

All research, development, and related activities involving human subjects and connected with the [Institution] must be approved by the [Board] *before* human subjects may be involved. All such research, development, and related activities conducted on the premises of the [Institution] are connected with the [Institution]. In addition, such activities conducted at sites other than the premises of the [Institution] are connected with the [Institution] if they (1) are funded through the [Institution], or (2) are conducted by faculty, medical staff members, students, or employees of the [Institution] who are acting in connection with their responsibilities or relationships to the [Institution] or who intend to use the name of the [Institution] in any report of the activity, or (3) involve the records of the [Institution], or (4) use the [Institution's] records, faculty, medical staff members, students, or employees to identify and/or contact its current clients, patients, or students to be subjects. For the purposes of this paragraph, a [Board] finding that there are no subjects at risk constitutes approval by the [Board]. [See section 11(e) of the protocol content part of this chapter for a discussion of the determination of whether subjects are at risk.]

Comment: This paragraph should state your institution's policy concerning the jurisdiction of the board. The paragraph should be identical to the jurisdictional paragraph developed after consideration of the discussion of some of the other possible policies concerning the jurisdiction of the board found in Chapter 3.

Where "Institution" or "Board" appears in brackets, you should substitute the name or appropriate reference that is most commonly used in your institution. Other terms and numbers that may have to be changed to fit the situation at your institution are placed in brackets throughout Chapters 2, 3, and 4.

Research, for the purposes of this [Board], is any process that seeks to secure new information from humans or about humans and that differs in any way from customary medical (or other professional) practice. The process need not be interactive; observation of humans through a one-way glass, by tape recording their conversations, or by examining their records may be classified as research within the ambit of the [Board's] responsibilities. The reorganization of old information in an effort to secure new information also constitutes research if it differs in any way from customary medical or professional practice. For example, extracting information by a retrospective search of medical records can constitute such a reorganization.

Comment: The boundary between research and professional practice is not always clear. For example, diagnostic tests are designed to secure new information, which can be useful for either research purposes or for the selection of therapy for the patient. The intent of the investigator or physician and the use to which the information is put may be the only way to determine whether the use of an established test constitutes research. For example, a physician conducting excessive tests to derive information to publish a more complete case report is conducting research.

One of the duties of the National Commission for the Protection of Human Subjects of Biomedical and Behavioral Research is to consider the boundary between research and practice. P. L. 93-348, Title II, §202(a)(1)(B)(i).

Development and related activities are those activities which, though not primarily research, have a research component. Whenever there is doubt whether an activity constitutes research or whether it has a research component, the [Chairman of the Board] should be consulted for a determination whether the [Board] should review the activity.

Protocols and consent forms must be completed according to these guidelines. They become part of the permanent records of the [Board] and, therefore, are subject to inspection and review by various funding and regulatory agencies. The specified information is necessary for the [Board] to conduct adequately the review that government regulations and the [Institution's] policies require. The [Board] will take no action on incomplete protocols and they will be returned to the investigator directly for revision.

Comment: If your institution adopts the policy of requiring prior review of protocols by a department chairman or another superior or administrator (see the comment on departmental level review in Chapter 3), the procedure for returning an incomplete protocol could be to transmit it to the investigator through the person responsible for prior review. This alternative procedure should aid the prior reviewer in assessing how well he is fulfilling his responsibility.

General Procedures

(1) The investigator shall prepare a complete protocol in conformity with these guidelines. The principal investigator shall sign the protocol.

(2) The investigator shall submit the completed protocol to the [Chairman of the Department] in which the research will be conducted for the [Chairman's] review and signature. If the research will not be conducted in a department, then the protocol should be submitted to the [Chairman of the Department] with which the investigator is associated. If neither of these applies, the [Chairman of the Board] should be consulted to determine who should conduct department level review.

Comment: This paragraph should be deleted if your institution decides not to require department level review.

This paragraph should communicate policy adopted after consideration of the suggestion and comment concerning department level review discussed in Chapter 3. The brackets reflect the fact that many institutions are organized in other ways and use other titles. The "Chairman of the Board" is in brackets to indicate that the responsibility for dealing with unusual situations could be allocated to someone with another title. An attempt could be made to detail all the possible situations; however, it would create an unnecessarily formidable paragraph.

(3) [Eight] copies of the completed protocol should be sent to the [Chairman of the Board] [Dr. _____ Room ___)]. At least one of the copies must be signed by both the principal investigator and the [Chairman of the Department]. If the study is to be funded by the DHEW, then [_____] copies of the full proposal should also be submitted.

Comment: Your institution might decide to have someone other than the chairman receive the protocols and distribute them to board members. The appropriate name and room should be given.

The reference to the signature of the department chairman should be deleted if the policy of your institution does not require his review. The number of copies appropriate for your institution should be inserted in the brackets. To determine the number of copies needed, count on one for each member of the board, one or more to file (depending on your institution's requirements), and one to return to the investigator with the appropriate signatures or transmittal memo.

The copies of the full proposal are for the primary and secondary reviewer (see Chapter 3 for a discussion of the responsibilities of the reviewers) and for the board's file. This permits the board to review the proposal itself to determine whether any relevant aspects have been overlooked in the protocol. This check is one approach to full compliance with the DHEW requirement of review of the proposed activity. It could also provide clarifying information that can preclude some of the questions raised by the protocol alone.

One danger of requiring submission of the full proposal is that investigators, instead of extracting salient information and putting it in the protocol submitted to the board, could merely make references in the protocol to pages of the full proposal. This makes the task of the board much more difficult. An alternative approach to requiring submission of the full proposal is to require the principal investigator to submit a signed statement certifying that all research involving human subjects in the full proposal is described in the protocol submitted to the board. If this approach is adopted, your institution will have to take strict action should it discover that an investigator has intentionally excluded a relevant part of a full proposal from a protocol.

(4) The [Board] will meet on the [second and fourth Wednesdays of each month]. Protocols received in the [Board chairman's] office by [noon] on the [Wednesday] preceding the next scheduled meeting will be reviewed at that meeting. Protocols received after [Wednesday noon] will be held over until the next subsequent meeting.

Comment: The frequency of board meetings will depend on the volume of research. Regular meetings permit every-

one—members and investigators—to plan their activities with
more ease. We suggest scheduling a regular meeting at least
monthly. This avoids the time-consuming and often nearly
impossible task of finding a mutually satisfactory time on short
notice. If no protocols are received by the deadline, the
members can be notified a week in advance that the scheduled
meeting is cancelled. This has the benefit of making membership on the board less of a burden.

The deadline also is necessary for the members to have
sufficient time to receive and examine the protocols. It permits
them to negotiate minor changes in the protocol or the consent
form with the investigator before the meeting. A longer period
of time between the deadline and the meeting may be desirable
to permit more careful examination and more resolutions of
difficulties. Two weeks for review would be an advantage.
However, as the period becomes longer than two weeks there
will be increasing pressure on the board to review protocols that
have missed the submission deadline.

A protocol might need revision and reconsideration before it can be
approved. If there is a deadline by which the research must be
approved to meet the requirements of a funding agency, the protocol
must be submitted sufficiently early to allow at least one scheduled
meeting remaining between the meeting at which the protocol is
first considered and the deadline.

When the protocol is likely to be controversial—for example, if it
involves high risk or particularly vulnerable subjects or matters about
which the community is particularly sensitive, it should be submitted
to allow at least two scheduled meetings remaining between the
meeting at which the protocol is first considered and the deadline.
Early submission will not guarantee approval by the deadline, but it
will increase the opportunity for discussion and resolution of issues
before the deadline.

Comment: The strictness of the deadlines is tempered somewhat
by the fact that under most circumstances certification of
review and approval by the board may be sent to the DHEW up
to ninety days after submission of an application or proposal for
support. The DHEW discourages such delays and will not review
the application or proposal until the certification is received. 40
Federal Register 22019 (May 20, 1975). We suggest that a
schedule of early submission to the board be followed. The
opportunity for delayed approval should be reserved for trouble-

some snags; it should not become part of the accepted procedure of the investigator or the board.

If there is any question concerning what constitutes a complete protocol after careful reading of the guidelines or if there is concern that the protocol could have controversial aspects, the [Board chairman] should be consulted for guidance.

Comment: Some other person or office may be designated for consultation. It should be one who is familiar with the policies and guidelines and with the way the board applies them, and one who is reasonably available.

(5) The chairman could request that the principal investigator be present at a portion of the [Board] meeting to provide information and answer questions. The investigator must be excused before the [Board] resumes deliberations concerning the protocol. The presence of the investigator will seldom be necessary because the protocol, supplemented by answers to the reviewers' questions, should provide all information that the [Board] needs. Even if his presence is not requested, the investigator should make a serious effort to be available when his protocol is on the [Board] agenda in the event the [Board] needs information only he can provide. This can be satisfied by providing the [Board] with a phone number at which he can be easily reached during the meeting. If his presence is necessary and he is unavailable, action will have to be postponed until the next meeting, to allow the opportunity for the investigator to be consulted.

For some purposes a member of the proposed study team might also have to be present to answer more specialized questions, but this should be rarely necessary.

Comment: The presence of the investigator is solely to facilitate the review by the board. It is not meant to be an opportunity for the investigator to give a lecture on his work. Boards that have to consider a large number of protocols could choose never to have an investigator present. If reviewers cannot resolve difficulties, then the board can appoint a subcommittee to examine the protocol with the investigator and then make a recommendation to the full board.

(6) [Board] approval is for a specific period of time, not greater than one year. If the [Board] decides that more frequent review is

necessary, it can choose to approve a study for a shorter period than the investigator desires. If involvement of human subjects in the study will continue longer than the period for which [Board] approval is granted, the investigator must resubmit the protocol (with a progress report) for reapproval.   Resubmission should be made promptly to avoid a gap in time during which the research must be stopped because the earlier approval has expired and reapproval has not yet been obtained. It should not be assumed that initial approval guarantees rapid reapproval.

(7) In the selection of potential subjects, prior professional relationships must be respected. If the study involves patients, then the personal physician must first determine that the patient is willing to discuss the study before the investigator can approach the patient. If the study involves clients, then the agency staff person who normally deals with the clients must first determine that the client is willing to discuss the study. If physicians or agencies merely provide the investigator with the names of those patients or clients with characteristics that make them eligible as subjects in the study, they are violating their confidential relationships.   Investigators should neither request nor accept the names unless they are assured that the patients or clients have agreed to be approached.

This problem also exists when access to records of persons with specified characteristics is sought. In most cases, the person to whom reference is made in the records should first be approached by the professional who generated the records or by the regular custodian of the records. This problem does not arise if the investigator is also the personal physician or normal staff contact. However, the problem of conflict of interest then arises, which may call for other special selection precautions, particularly if the risks to the subjects of the study are substantial.

(8) The investigator must give each subject a copy of the consent form or written summary to keep, unless the [Board] waives the requirement. [The written summary is used when oral consent is obtained. See section (11)(d) of the protocol content part of this chapter.]

Comment: This is not required by current federal regulations. See 39 *Federal Register* 18915, comment H (May 30, 1974). However, we suggest that your institution require a copy for the subject. It helps the subject to maintain continuing understanding of his involvement in the research and can help avoid some problems should a subject forget that he has been informed previously of a risk or discomfort. Also, the form or summary assists the subject to recognize differences between his actual experience and what was expected.   He can bring any discrepancies to the attention of the investigator, especially when the consent form facilitates such contact by providing the name and telephone number of the investigator to contact.   This allows prompt responses to developing difficulties and discovery of effects that could otherwise be missed. The approach can also contribute to preserving a good relationship between investigator and subject.

It would be reasonable for the board to waive this requirement when a study involves little risk and the subject will only be contacted once. An example of such a study is one requiring the taking of a single blood sample. If your institution decides not to make this a requirement, we suggest that the paragraph be modified and put into the language of a recommendation to investigators.

(9) Unless the study only involves an interview and/or the completion of a questionnaire, there must be a forty-eight-hour time period between when the potential subject is informed about the study and when a decision whether to participate is solicited, unless the [Board] approves a shorter time period. (See section (11)(c) of the protocol content part of this chapter.)

Comment: This is not required by current federal regulations. See 39 *Federal Register* 18915, comment H (May 30, 1974). However, we suggest that it be adopted as institutional policy. It permits and encourages the potential subject to take time to consider his decision and provides an opportunity for him to discuss participation with relatives, friends, and his personal medical advisor.   It can reduce the pressure on the potential subject to participate.

The forty-eight-hour delay is not necessary for minimal risk studies that involve a single contact with the subject.   Since many studies are of this type, it will not be unusual for the board to approve a shorter time period. One example of a more than minimal risk study for which the board might approve a shorter time period is one involving the prompt treatment of a traumatic injury. Of course, this situation could present special problems in obtaining effective consent because of the effects of pain and medication on the patient. Other precautions may be required. If your institution decides not to make this a requirement, we suggest that the paragraph be modified and put into the language of a recommendation to investigators.

(10) [Board] approval is only for the study described in the protocol. If the investigator desires to modify the study, he must obtain [Board] approval of the modified protocol before involving human subjects in the modified study.

(11) Unexpected situations could develop requiring the consent form to be modified or the study to be modified or suspended. If the investigator encounters injuries or inconveniences to the subjects of his studies that were not listed in the protocol or if he encounters a larger incidence of a particular injury or inconvenience than was indicated in the protocol, he must notify the [Board] promptly. The [Board] may require modifications of the consent form or other parts of the protocol before the study can be continued.

Protocol Content

An investigator must be designated to receive communications concerning the protocol. The individual so designated must be someone who can be expected to be available during the entire period of the study and, therefore, will not necessarily be the principal investigator.

(1) *Purpose.* This should be a brief statement of what the investigator seeks to learn from the study. This can often be stated as an hypothesis.

(2) *Background.* This should be a statement that describes past experimental and/or clinical findings leading to the formulation of the particular study, one which is comprehensible without reference to other materials.

(3) *Sources of funds.* This should state the names of the governmental agencies, foundations, corporations, other organizations, and individuals contributing to the funding of the research, with the percentage of the total funds each is expected to contribute.

(4) *Type and number of experimental subjects and controls.* This should include both an estimate of the number of subjects and controls involved as well as a statement describing the population from which they will be derived (for example, pregnant inpatients, outpatients with a specific disease, researchers, students, etc.).

The subjects that the investigator is studying may not be the only subjects at risk. For example, when venereal disease or contraception is involved, the sexual partner of the subject being studied could also be a subject at risk. Such subjects also should be indicated.

If the population includes special groups such as prisoners, children, the mentally disabled, or groups whose ability to give consent may be in question, the reasons for using such subjects must be included. If the objective of the study can be met through the use of competent, noninstitutionalized adults, the [Board] cannot approve the use of special groups. (Studies of the effects of an agent or procedure on special groups should be preceded by studies of its effects on competent, noninstitutional adults, unless the study involves only small risks and the condition that the agent or procedure is intended to affect is of markedly greater frequency or severity in the special group. Such prior studies should be described in the section on background.)

Comment: The use of subjects other than competent, non-institutionalized adults raises consent issues that have not been fully resolved. The policy options are discussed in the comment on special populations in Chapter 3. This paragraph should be written to express the policies adopted there.

(5) *Location of study.* This should specify the location where the contact with the subjects will occur. If it is a field study, the community in which the study is to be conducted should be described. Otherwise, the name of the institution should be given and the type of room described, e.g., Intensive Care Unit of the [State Medical Center], Emergency Room of [Memorial Hospital], [Metropolitan] Family Planning Clinic.

Comment: The examples should be specific and familiar to investigators in your institution. The location helps the board to assess the atmosphere in which the potential subject will be approached. It may alert them to the need for special precautions.

(6) *Probable duration.* This should include an estimate of the duration of the entire study. Since this estimate will be used to establish the period for which the study will be approved, the estimate should be a liberal one so the investigator can avoid being required to resubmit the study for an extension if it happens to be prolonged. There should also be an estimate of the total amount of time each subject will be involved. If a subject's involvement in the study will involve several phases, such as a sequence of treatments

and follow-up contacts, estimate the duration of each of the phases if it is not clear from the description of the study methodology below.

(7) *Description of the study methodology.* This section is addressed to the [Board] (in contrast with the consent form, which is addressed to the subject). There should be a description of the intended experimental procedure as it affects the subjects. There need not be a detailed account of experimental techniques that do not directly affect the subject, but those aspects of the proposed research that might cause subjects inconvenience, danger, or discomfort must be specified. The length of time that various procedures will take and the frequency with which they will be repeated must also be specified. If an interview or questionnaire is utilized in the study, a copy of the interview outline or questionnaire must be appended to the protocol.

(8) *Possible risks.* Describe all potential risks (physical, psychological, and social) with some estimate (based on past experience of the investigator or others) of their frequency, severity, and reversibility.

(9) *Special precautions.* This section should include any precautions that will be taken to avoid hazards, the means for monitoring to detect hazards, and the point at which the experiment will be terminated if these hazards materialize. There will probably be different threshholds for the termination of the involvement of an individual subject and for the termination of the entire study. There should also be specific statements describing the method of screening potential subjects and controls, and the factors that will be the basis for excluding potential subjects from the study.

In studies where the effectiveness of an agent or therapy is being assessed, the protocol should indicate the point at which the differences in outcomes between subjects and controls will be considered sufficiently significant to eliminate the need for additional subjects, or to require modification of the disclosure made to continuing and prospective subjects because of greater information concerning relative risks.

If, at the time the information concerning the research is presented to the potential subject and his consent is solicited, the potential subject will be, or recently has been, in a stressful, painful, or drugged condition, this fact should be specifically indicated in this section, along with the proposed precautions to overcome the effect of the condition on the consent process.

(10) *Procedures to maintain confidentiality.* Procedures for maintaining confidentiality of the data and the identity of the subjects and controls must be set forth. If the study calls for the

furnishing of information derived from the study to the subject, his personal physician, a governmental agency, or any other person or group, this section must describe to whom information will be given and the nature of the information, in addition to the description of the procedures for maintaining confidentiality as to others. Such disclosures are not breaches of confidentiality as long as the individual has given his consent to them.

> **Comment:** To aid the investigator and facilitate review, an institution might choose to describe two or three basic procedures for maintaining confidentiality here. If the investigator chose to use one of those procedures, he would then only have to state which basic procedure he was using, describing any modifications he may have made.

(11) *Other information.* Any other information that the investigator believes the [Board] should possess to assist it in fulfilling its responsibilities should be included. In the usual situation (where all necessary information is included in other sections) write "none." The following items should be included in this section whenever they are applicable:

(a) Investigators should be scientifically qualified to conduct the research and, where there are medical risks, the research should be conducted under the supervision of a qualified medical practitioner. If the qualifications of the investigators are not well known to the [Board] they should be indicated in this section. If medical supervision is necessary the name of the responsible physician should be given, along with a telephone number at which he can be reached.

> **Comment:** Basic Principle I.2 of the Declaration of Helsinki of the World Medical Association provides that clinical research "should be conducted only by scientifically qualified persons and under the supervision of a qualified medical man."

Some studies might require that the investigator or a member of his staff have special qualifications—for example, knowledge of how to handle immediately the occurrence of certain reactions that are known risks of the study. If special qualifications are necessary this section should include the name of the person and sufficient information to substantiate the qualifications.

> **Comment:** Your institution may want to establish more specific criteria for when a responsible physician must be designated.

(b) If other review boards have reviewed the study, give the current status of their determinations, e.g., pending, approved, or rejected. If rejected, give reasons.

When a field study is to be undertaken within a particular racial, religious, or geographical community, the nature and extent of preliminary contacts, if any, with community representatives to determine acceptance of the study by the community should be set forth. Similarly, if the study is to be undertaken within a school, business, or other institution that does not have a review board, preliminary contacts, if any, with appropriate officials should be set forth.

Comment: One of the board's functions is to assess community attitudes concerning the acceptability of the proposed study. The report of preliminary contacts can aid this assessment and should be encouraged because they permit more direct community involvement and assessment. Also, they can help avoid potential embarrassments, such as charges of exploitation.

(c) In the event that a new drug is to be used or that an old drug is to be used for a new (nonapproved) purpose, it should be stated that the appropriate forms and information have been filed with the FDA or—if applicable—that the FDA has waived jurisdiction for the specific study.

Comment: Alternatively, the policy of actually reviewing the documents can be adopted. If so, replace the language after "purpose" with "copies of the forms and information filed with the FDA shall be submitted as part of the protocol." However, it might not be necessary for the full board to review the documents. If so, only one copy of the FDA documents would be required. They would be reviewed by the chairman or another designated member knowledgeable about drugs, who would report to the full board.

Legislation creating similar federal regulation of new medical devices has been pending in Congress for several years. It has been given increasingly serious attention but has not yet been enacted. If it should be enacted, it would need mention here.

(d) If the investigator proposes a time period between informing the subject and soliciting a decision that is less than forty-eight hours, he must describe the time sequence he desires and the reasons why the forty-eight-hour minimum would handicap the effective conduct of the study or would be disadvantageous to the subject. One sufficient reason for a shorter time period would be that the study involves minimal risk and/or a single contact with the subject.

Comment: If the institution chose not to adopt a policy of requiring this time period, this paragraph would be deleted.

(e) If the [Board] determines that there are no subjects "at risk,"* then the DHEW regulations impose no additional requirements. If the investigator seeks a determination that there are no subjects at risk, there should be a request for such a determination in this section. If any additional information could help demonstrate that there are no subjects at risk, it should be presented here.

However, risk is so broadly defined that few investigations involving humans would not put them "at risk." For example, if blood removed from the body for therapeutic reasons is used for an additional diagnostic test to determine whether the subject has a socially embarrassing condition (venereal disease or a genetic abnormality), the subject is at risk—despite the absence of any physical risk. Questionnaires raising issues that might be emotionally disturbing or might elicit potentially embarrassing information also place the subject at risk. Thus, an investigator should be seeking socially neutral information through methods that add no risk of physical or psychological injury before he requests a determination that the subjects are not at risk.

No consent form need be included in such a protocol. However, the investigator would be well advised to include a proposed consent form so, if the [Board] determines that the subjects are at risk, deliberations will not have to be postponed until a subsequent meeting. The portion of the consent form dealing with risks can be left blank. The [Board] can then add a description of the risks it identifies.

Even though there might be no legal requirement to obtain consent when there are no risks, investigators should seriously consider obtaining consent out of respect for human dignity. Studies involving no risk should be the ones in which subjects will most readily participate, knowingly and willingly.

---

* "Subject at risk" means any individual who may be exposed to the possibility of injury, including physical, psychological, or social injury, as a consequence of participation as a subject in any research, development, or related activity which departs from the application of those established and accepted methods necessary to meet his needs, or which increases the ordinary risks of daily life, including the recognized risks inherent in a chosen occupation or field of service. 45 C.F.R. §46.103(b).

(f) There are three possible approaches to documentation of consent of the subject. The preferred approach is to use the written consent form; its preparation is described in these guidelines. If the investigator believes that the study qualifies for one of the other two approaches, [Board] approval may be requested for use of that approach. The specific reasons why that approach should be approved should be given in this section of the protocol.

The *short form* written consent requires that

(i)   the subject and an auditor-witness sign a statement that the subject has been orally informed about the research,

(ii) a written summary of what is to be said to the potential subject be approved by the [Board], and

(iii) the investigator and the auditor-witness both sign a copy of the summary, annotated to show any additions, certifying that all information in the summary was presented to the subject. See 45 C.F.R. §46.110(b).

If this approach is desired, the protocol should include a copy of the written summary in place of the written consent form. The written summary must include *all* information required to be provided a subject when the written consent form is employed. It is the policy of the [Institution] to prefer written consent; therefore, the investigator must establish that employing the short form would be advantageous to the subject.

A *modified procedure* may be approved if three conditions are all demonstrated:

(i)   the risk to any subject is minimal,

(ii) objectives of considerable immediate importance would be surely invalidated by using either written or short form written consent, and

(iii) any reasonable alternative means for attaining these objectives would be less advantageous to the subjects. See 45 C.F.R. §46.110(c).

If this approach is desired the protocol should include the details of the desired modification and evidence that the three conditions are met.

Comment: Current federal regulations do not indicate a preference for the written consent document. The short form written consent document is given equal status; no special showing is required to justify its use. However, we suggest that your institution adopt the policy of preferring the written consent document. We feel that, if the consent is later challenged, written consent provides stronger evidence that the subject was informed before consent was given. Of course, many subjects actually pay more attention to information presented orally. Thus, written consent should not supplant the investigator's oral explanation. The prudent investigator will both explain the study orally and use the full written consent document. The written consent document can also benefit the subject by offering him an opportunity to examine an explanation that has been independently determined to be accurate and complete. It avoids inadvertent omissions. For some subjects, the document might also communicate the importance of the decision better, focusing more of the subject's attention on the information and the decision.

Covert observation, participant observation, and deception studies present particular difficulties. Some authorities maintain that an informed consent to not being informed of certain aspects of the study is effective, especially when the general nature of the withheld information is disclosed. Apparently, DHEW has approved deception studies using this approach. However, the language of the regulations calls for "knowing consent" and specifies the "basic elements of information necessary to such consent," which could be interpreted to disallow such studies. It could also be possible for some studies of this nature to be fit within the requirements of subsection (f) for modified procedures for obtaining consent. However, this is not certain. If your institution is involved in this type of research, it might desire to adopt a separate policy concerning procedures for such research. (See the discussion of such psychological and social science research in Chapter 3). If the institution decides to authorize modified procedures under circumstances other than those listed in subsection (f), it should describe those circumstances in another subsection.

Written Consent Form

The most common reason for delay of approval of a protocol is an inadequate consent form. The consent form should be a statement addressed to the subject and should read as such. Ordinarily it is best worded in the second person; it must be in language the subject can understand. This includes avoiding or defining technical terminology, adjusting for educational background, and providing translations into other languages when some of the anticipated subject population does not understand English.

When consent of the legal representative is necessary in addition to or instead of the consent of the subject, the consent form language discussed in this chapter must be modified to indicate that consent is being solicited from a person other than the subject.

Comment: Federal regulations do not require that consent forms be written in the second person. We suggest that the institution adopt this approach as its policy because, combined with the conditional language ("if", "then") and the invitation to participate, it best communicates that the investigator believes that there is a choice to be made. The more traditional first person approach is written as if the reader has already decided to participate and, thus, makes it more difficult for the potential subject to decline participation. This sort of subtle influence should be avoided.

If the institution decides not to adopt this policy, we suggest that it recommend and encourage the use of second person consent forms.

Because there is so much information to present, an effort should be made to be concise. It is preferable for the entire document to be on one side of a single paper. If this is not possible, it should be on both sides of a single sheet rather than on two sheets. In the rare circumstance where additional space is necessary, there should be a place for the subject to initial the sheets on which his signature does not appear.

Comment: Subjects often forget information presented to them. This does not reduce the legal effectiveness of their consent, but it can lead to later assertions that they were not given the information. Multiple page consent forms invite an assertion that one or more of the pages were not presented to the subject. The suggestions above are designed to facilitate proof later that all information was made available.

The checklist of points to be covered in the written consent form, which appears below, applies to all kinds of research. Some points, as indicated, might not apply to every study. Behavioral research, especially, might require a different emphasis on some points.

The checklist is numbered, but those numbers should not appear on the consent form.

(1) A statement of the general purpose of the study.

Comment: DHEW regulations only require inclusion of the purposes of the procedures to be followed.   45 C.F.R. §46.103(c)(1). We suggest that the purpose of the study be disclosed because, without this knowledge, the subject can neither assess the importance of the study within his value system nor be a full participant in the study.

(2) An invitation to participate. Points (1) and (2) can be combined in language such as: "You are invited to participate in a study of....   We hope to learn...." Alternatively, the second sentence could begin: "We hope that this study will help us to...."

Comment: The invitation to participate is not required by DHEW regulations. We suggest that the invitation be used because it helps to communicate that there is a choice to be made.

(3) Why this subject was selected, e.g., because he is a normal adult male, has asthma, or has relatives with a specific disease. If the statement of purpose of the study identifies the subject population, it need not be repeated here.

Comment: DHEW regulations do not require including the reason for selection. We suggest that the selection criteria be disclosed because it helps the subject to assess the nature and importance of his participation.

(4) Describe the procedures to be followed, including their purposes, how long they will take, and their frequency. Use of randomization or placebos should be disclosed. If any of the procedures are experimental, they must be identified as such. For purposes of this special identification, a *procedure* is experimental if there has not been sufficient experience with it to establish a general professional consensus concerning the risks of its use in circumstances similar to those of the study. This section should begin with: "If you decide to participate, we will...."

Comment: DHEW regulations require the inclusion of "a fair explanation of the procedures to be followed, and their purposes, including identification of any procedures which are experimental." §46.103(c)(1). The above interpretation of "experimental procedure" is our own; there are other possible interpretations. For example, any procedure not professionally accepted for therapeutic or diagnostic purposes could be considered experimental. However, we feel that a well-understood procedure is no longer an experimental procedure, even if it has no accepted therapeutic or diagnostic use. This maintains the distinction between an experimental procedure and an experimental use of a procedure. This discussion is directed only to the issue of when the special label "experimental procedure" must be applied. Whether or not a procedure is an "experimental procedure," if the procedure is being used for experimental purposes it must be described in the consent form. Of course, any use of an experimental procedure is an experimental use.

(5) Describe the discomforts and inconveniences that might be reasonably expected. An estimate of the total amount of the subject's time required must be included if it is not clear from the procedure description. For example: "This study will take seven periods of approximately two hours each. The periods will be in seven consecutive weeks."

Comment: DHEW regulations require the inclusion of "a description of any attendant discomforts and risks reasonably to be expected." §46.103(c)(2). We add "inconveniences" because they are a form of discomfort that might otherwise be overlooked. Also, many subjects may be more upset by inconveniences than by other discomforts.

(6) If there are any risks of involvement, describe them. Merely writing "minimal risks" is not enough.

Comment: As quoted in the previous comment, DHEW regulations require a description of the attendant risks. The many court decisions concerning informed consent in nonresearch medical contexts will certainly be cited whenever a court must determine whether sufficient disclosure existed. The standard being widely adopted is that the patient must be given any information that a reasonable person in the position of the patient would want to know before reaching a decision on whether to consent. This has been tempered by a "therapeutic privilege" not to disclose information in some circumstances. The physician has the burden of demonstrating the reasonableness of his belief that those circumstances exist. Thus, the scope of the privilege is probably limited. It is also probably necessary to disclose any information encompassed by a therapeutic privilege to the patient's family or other legally authorized representative, if available. [For a court discussion, see *Canterbury v. Spence*, 464 F.2d 772, 789 (D. C. Cir. 1972).] The subject is in a different position than the patient. He is being exposed to risks that are less predictable and that are not solely for his direct benefit. Thus, the subject needs to know more than the patient. When a therapeutic procedure is part of a study, the subject is exposed to both the risks of the procedure and the risks of the study. He may choose to accept the risks of the procedure, but not the risks of participation in the study. There is no therapeutic privilege not to disclose information to a subject.   Several states, for example Idaho, have recently enacted laws to deal with the malpractice situation, reducing the duty to inform patients; these statutes do not reduce the duty to inform research subjects.

(7) If any benefits to the subject can reasonably be expected, they should be described. Many studies have no benefits to the subject. Some benefits might be asserted for subjects, but they would not be sufficiently supported for the [Board] to find the expectation of their occurrence appropriate for inclusion in the consent form.   The suggestion of a benefit can be a strong inducement to participation, so it should be limited to substantial and likely benefits. If the benefits to controls are different from the benefits to other subjects, this should be made clear. If benefits are mentioned, it should be made clear that the researcher cannot and does not make any guarantee that the benefits will necessarily occur.

Comment: DHEW regulations require the inclusion of "a description of any benefits reasonably to be expected." §46.103(c)(3).

(8) If any standard treatment is being withheld, it should be disclosed. If there are any other appropriate alternative procedures that might be advantageous to the subject, describe them.
"Appropriate" and "advantageous" should be interpreted in terms of the spectrum of responsible professional judgment, not by the investigator's personal professional judgment alone. If other members of the investigator's profession would consider an alternative

appropriate and advantageous, the investigator should mention it, notwithstanding his personal opinion to the contrary. He may, of course, mention the reasons for his opinion.

Comment: DHEW regulations require "a disclosure of any appropriate alternative procedures that might be advantageous for the subject." §46.103(c)(4). We call special attention to standard treatments that are being withheld because such treatments are usually the subject's primary alternative to being involved in the research.

(9) Confidentiality: if data obtained will be made available to any person or organization other than the subject, the investigator, and the investigator's staff, the persons or agencies to whom information will be furnished, the purpose of the disclosure, and the nature of the information to be furnished must be described. This section should begin: "Any information that is obtained in connection with this study and that could identify you will remain confidential and will be disclosed only with your permission. If you give us your permission by signing this document, we plan to disclose...."

Comment: DHEW regulations provide that "except as otherwise provided by law, information in the records or possession of the institution acquired in connection with an activity covered by this part, which information refers to or can be identified with a particular subject, may not be disclosed except: (1) with the consent of the subject or his legally authorized representative; or (2) as may be necessary for the Secretary to carry out his responsibilities under this part." §46.119(b). Thus, it is not required that a promise of confidentiality appear in the consent document. However, some subjects may be more likely to consent knowing that information is confidential. Written consent for the disclosure of information should be obtained, either in this written consent document or in a separate consent document.

Data in the form of tape recordings, photographs, movies, or videotapes will require special attention. If such records will be made, they should be described, regardless of whether they will be shown to others. The maximum period of time they will be retained before destruction should also be disclosed.

Showing or playing such data for any purpose must be disclosed. They can be shown or played only in the situations to which the subject consented. Special attention should be paid to disclosing all showing or playing for instructional purposes. There is always the possibility that someone in the audience will recognize the subject in a visual recording. Because of the significant social risks to the subject, the investigator should exercise considerable discretion, even when consent to the showing has been obtained.

If a subject can participate in the study without having information on audio or visual recordings shown to others, that fact should be disclosed. This can be accomplished either by indicating that the subject may cross out the portion of the consent form dealing with disclosure to others or by preparing a separate document for consent to disclosure to others.

Comment: The DHEW regulations do not directly address audio or visual recordings; however, we recommend paying special attention to them because of the duty to assure that the rights of subjects are adequately protected. Unauthorized use would constitute a significant invasion of the right of privacy, which could have substantial emotional and economic consequences.

(10) Compensation and costs: if the subject will receive payment, the amount must be described or stated. If subjects receive services or treatment at a lower cost than would be charged nonsubjects, the reduction in cost is a form of compensation for participating in the study. If there is the potential of additional cost to the subject from participation in the study, it must be disclosed.

Comment: DHEW regulations do not specifically require mention of compensation, although the required disclosure of benefits can be interpreted to include compensation. We suggest that promises of compensation should be put in writing here because it will help avoid potential disagreements over terms. In addition, this permits the board to determine whether the compensation constitutes the "undue inducement" prohibited by the regulations. §46.103(c).

(11) Indicate that the subject is free to decide not to participate or, later, to withdraw his consent and discontinue participation in the study, without prejudice. For example: "Your decision whether or not to participate will not prejudice your future relations with the [Institution] and [the named cooperating institution or agency, if any]. If you decide to participate, you are free to withdraw your consent and to discontinue participation at any time without prejudice."

Comment: DHEW regulations require "an instruction that the person is free to withdraw his consent and to discontinue participation at any time without prejudice to the subject." §46.103(c)(6). Prejudice refers to such matters as future care, reimbursement of expenses, compensation, and employment status (see 39 *Federal Register* 18914, Comment c, May 30, 1974). In most circumstances, this probably does not preclude conditioning a portion of the payment on the completion of involvement, as long as that is clearly stated. We suggest adding that the subject is free to decide not to participate because this contributes to the whole thrust of emphasizing that the subject has been presented a choice.

(12) Offer to answer any inquires concerning the procedures of the study. Include the name and phone number or address of an investigator that the subject can contact, if he has any further question. Serveral tones are possible. For example:
(a) "We will answer any questions you have about the study;" or
(b) "Feel free to ask any questions you have about the study, and we will be happy to answer them;" or
(c) "If you have any questions, we expect you to ask us."
Each of these sentences should be followed by: "If you have any additional questions later, [name] [provide a phone number or address where he can be reached] will be happy to answer them."

Comment: DHEW regulations require "an offer to answer any inquiries concerning the procedures." §46.103(c)(5). We have suggested language to help the investigator encourage inquiries.

We suggest that any additional information that is given to subjects in response to their questions be noted, either in their medical records or in the file concerning their participation in the study.

Following the offer to answer inquiries, the following sentence should appear: "You will be given a copy of this form to keep."

Comment: If the institution decides to not require that the subject be given a copy of the consent form, then this sentence should be deleted.

(13) Conclude with: "You are making a decision whether or not to participate. Your signature indicates that you have decided to participate having read the information provided above."

Comment: There are several approaches to the language expressing the subject's decision to participate. We suggest the above approach because we believe that it simply and clearly expresses that a decision is being made. Additional words expressing that the subject "understands" are self-serving and do not add the intended extra protection for the investigator or the institution. Instead, they tend to introduce a legalistic tone we wish to avoid. However, since there is still room for disagreement, we offer one alternative incorporating such language: "You are making a decision whether or not to participate. Your signature on this document indicates that you have read and understand the information provided above, that you have decided to participate, and that you consent to the procedures or treatment described above." There is one clear constraint on the approach taken. The DHEW regulations prohibit any exculpatory language. 45 C.F.R. §46.109.

If the subject is legally incompetent, requiring a parent or other legal representative to decide, then the suggested language should be changed to: "You are making a decision whether or not ___ _____ will participate. Your signature indicates that, having read the information provided above, you have decided to permit _____ to participate." Similar changes should be made in the alternative language.

In some circumstances, state regulations may require that the concluding paragraph include specific language. For example, in Massachusetts consent forms for research with controlled substances must conclude with a statement that the subject has read and understands the "Statement of Informed Consent," that he understands he may terminate his consent at any time, and that he voluntarily consents to be a subject of the described project. §9.5.2, Regulations under Mass. Gen. Laws Ann. Chap. 94C. Such requirements, of course, must be complied with.

(14) Below the foregoing paragraph there must be space for signatures and the date and time of signature. If the subject is legally competent, he must sign the form. If he is not legally competent, (e.g., a minor, a mentally disabled person, or otherwise under guardianship), his guardian or parent must sign the form after receiving the explanation of the study. There should be a space for the signer to indicate his relationship to the subject. In some circumstances the [Board] might require that the signature of the

incompetent also be obtained, e.g., older minors and those with limited mental disabilities. Where both the subject and his legal representative are to provide consent, two separate forms will be necessary. The person who actually explained the study and interacted with the subject in the consent process should sign the form. This person need not always be the investigator. The investigator can delegate the function of soliciting consent to anyone who is capable of answering questions from the subjects. This delegation does not reduce the investigator's responsibility to obtain effective informed consent, however. Another person who actually witnessed the signing of the form by the subject or his legally authorized representative should also sign the form. If possible, the witness should be someone who is not otherwise involved in the study. The bottom of the form should appear as follows:

_____
Date

                        AM
                        PM
_____
Time

                    _____
                    Signature

                    _____
                    Relationshop to subject
                    [This line should not appear on forms that will
                    be given to subjects consenting for them-
                    selves.]

_____   _____
Signature of Witness   Signature of Investigator

Comment: Federal regulations require only the signature of the subject or his legally authorized representative and do not require the signature of the investigator or of a witness. We recommend the signature of the investigator so it can be established who discussed the study with the subject. This is particularly important in a situation where there are several investigators involved in one study. We recommend the signature of a person unconnected with the study as a witness so, if necessary, the condition of the subject can be established. If the subject is a hospital patient, another approach to documentation is to write a description of the subject's condition in the medical chart or nurse's notes. The date and the time, in conjunction with the medical chart, help to indicate whether the subject was alert enough to make an adequate decision. The question of under what circumstances the consent of an incompetent person should also be obtained remains unsettled. Until there are other authoritative decisions, the board should establish its own policy (see the discussion of special populations in Chapter 3). As that policy evolves, it should be presented in these guidelines.

An institution might choose to place limits on whom an investigator may delegate the function of soliciting consent to avoid delegation to inappropriate people. Any such decision should be reflected in this paragraph.

SUGGESTED ADDITIONAL PROCEDURES

Some investigators might desire to take additional steps to assure that the subjects are informed and are making voluntary decisions. The board might decide to require such additional steps when studies are particularly controversial, for example, when they involve high risk, particularly vulnerable subjects, or matters about which the community is particularly sensitive. In addition, the Secretary of the DHEW might impose additional conditions to any grant or contract when in his judgment they are necessary for the protection of human subjects. 45 C.F.R. §46.122. Some of the steps which have been proposed or tried are discussed below.

Expecting Negative Decisions

One British investigator always aims for rejections from at least a certain percentage of the people from whom he solicits consent. He feels that if everyone approached consents he has failed to explain the risks adequately. Although not conclusive, the fact that some people decided not to participate is evidence that the presentation was fair and did not put undue pressure on potential subjects to consent. We suggest that each investigator keep a record of such refusals.

Questioning by the Investigator

After explaining the study and having the potential subject read the consent form, the investigator can ask questions about the study. Thus, the investigator can satisfy himself that the subject has understood the explanation before offering the form for signature.

The Two-Part Consent Form

Instead of (or in addition to) having the investigator ask questions, the potential subject can be given a short questionnaire concerning the study. Until the subject can answer the questions correctly, he should not be permitted to sign the consent form. The completed questionnaire would be filed with the signed consent form. Among other benefits, this provides better evidence that the subject understood. [For further discussion, see R. D. Miller and H. S. Willner, "The Two-Part Consent Form," *New England Journal of Medicine*, Vol. 290: 964 (April 25, 1974).]

Tape Recording and Videotaping

The explanation to the subject and the rest of the consent process can be tape recorded or videotaped. This provides evidence of exactly what was said. It is expensive to make and retain such recordings, but for sensitive studies the cost might be well worthwhile. If proper consent is obtained, such recordings are also useful to study and teach the consent process.

Subject Advocates

The presence of a subject-advocate during the consent process may be useful. This is especially true if many members of the subject population are in awe of the investigators, are likely to be influenced easily, or have limited capacity to ask appropriate questions.

Consent Committees

A consent committee is useful when it is necessary to assess carefully the comprehension of the subject and the pressures on the subject to consent. Such committees were included in the proposed DHEW regulations dealing with several categories of subjects considered in need of particular protection (see §§46.305, 46.405, 46.506, 46.62, 39 *Federal Register*, 30653-30656, August 23, 1974). The regulations were never promulgated, but such committees have been tried. For example, one was established by Boston City Hospital for the potential subjects of psychosurgery. The Oregon legislature has established a Psychosurgery Review Board that, among other duties, performs this function.

Follow-Up

In addition to any follow-up necessary for the study design, the investigator can contact the subject several weeks after the end of the subject's participation to determine the subject's condition and his feelings about participation in the study. This can catch delayed reactions and dissatisfactions and enable action to reduce the likelihood of possible charges or litigation.

See Protocol Format, pages 44 through 46.

PROTOCOL FORMAT

Protocol for Research Study

[Institution]

Title of Study:
Principal Investigator:
Other Investigators:
Department (or Departments):

                                   _____   _____

                                    Signature of   Date
                                          Principal Investigator

_____

Name of Investigator to
Receive Communications   _____   _____
Concerning this Protocol   Signature of   Date
                                        Department Chairman

_____

Address

_____

(Space Below for Board use)

Date Approved: _____   _____
                              Signature of Board Chairman

Period of Approval: _____

*   *   *

[Page 2, and as many additional pages as necessary:]

Description of Study

1. Purpose:
2. Background:
3. Sources of Funds:
4. Type and Number of Experimental Subjects and Controls:
5. Location of Study:
6. Probable Duration:
7. Description of the Study Methodology:
8. Possible Risks:
9. Special Precautions:
10. Procedures to Maintain Confidentiality:
11. Other Information:

Subject Consent for Participation in an Investigation

[Institution]

You are invited to participate in a study of [state what is being studied]. We hope to learn [state what the study is designed to discover or establish]. You were selected as a possible participant in this study because [state why the subject was selected].

If you decide to participate, we [or: Dr. _____ and his associates] will [describe the procedures to be followed, including their purposes, how long they will take, and their frequency]. [Describe the discomforts and inconveniences reasonably to be expected. An estimate of the total time required must be included.] [Describe the risks reasonably to be expected.] [Describe any benefits reasonably to be expected. If benefits are mentioned, add:] We cannot and do not guarantee or promise that you will receive any benefits from this study.

[Describe appropriate alternative procedures that might be advantageous to the subject, if any. Any standard treatment that is being withheld must be disclosed.]

Any information that is obtained in connection with this study and that can be identified with you will remain confidential and will be disclosed only with your permission. If you give us your permission by signing this document, we plan to disclose [state the persons or agencies to whom the information will be furnished, the nature of the information to be furnished, and the purpose of the disclosure].

[If the subject will receive compensation, describe the amount or nature.] [If there is a possibility of additional costs to the subject because of participation, describe it.]

Your decision whether or not to participate will not prejudice your future relations with the [Institution] [and the named cooperating institution, if any]. If you decide to participate, you are free to withdraw your consent and to discontinue participation at any time without prejudice.

If you have any questions, we expect you to ask us. If you have any additional questions later, Dr. _____ , (give a phone number or address) will be happy to answer them.

You will be given a copy of this form to keep.

YOU ARE MAKING A DECISION WHETHER OR NOT TO PARTICIPATE. YOUR SIGNATURE INDICATES THAT YOU HAVE DECIDED TO PARTICIPATE HAVING READ THE INFORMATION PROVIDED ABOVE.

_____
Date

               AM
_____PM
Time

_____
Signature

_____
Relationship to subject
[This line should not appear on forms that will be given to subjects consenting for them-selves.]

_____   _____
Singature of Witness   Signature of Investigator

3

RESPONSIBILITIES OF THE INSTITUTIONAL REVIEW BOARD

There are many aspects of each proposed study for the board to consider. We suggest that each board develop a framework for review that enables it to focus consideration on specific issues, to assist in maintaining a consistent decision-making policy, and to delineate responsibilities. This chapter is designed to aid in the development of such a framework. Many issues will be raised that require a decision concerning which approach your institution will take. These decisions can be left for the board to make as the issues arise; or they can be addressed by the institutional authorities, thereby establishing general policies.

Rather than designing this chapter to be a draft document with drafting comments, here we will discuss issues in a decision-making framework. Only three draft documents are included in this chapter: (1) a jurisdictional statement, (2) a procedure for protocol submission, and (3) a procedure for the conduct of the deliberations of the board, with an accompanying statement of the duties of the members of the board.

RESEARCH CONCERNS OF THE BOARD

To delineate the responsibilities of the board and to alert investigators to the studies they must bring to the board for approval,

47

it is necessary for each institution to adopt a policy concerning which studies must be reviewed by the board.

The DHEW regulations require this review only for research, development, and related activities involving human subjects that are funded by DHEW. 45 C.F.R. §46.102(a).* The FDA provides for board review of some research with Investigational New Drugs. 21 C.F.R. §312.1. Some state laws and regulations require review in some circumstances. (See Chapter 5.) These specific requirements establish the the minimum jurisdiction of the board. The concern of the DHEW with the interests of subjects is not confined solely to the research that it funds. Failure to protect the rights and welfare of subjects of unfunded research and research funded by other sources can jeopardize the eligibility of both the investigator and the institution to receive future DHEW grants and contracts that involve the use of human subjects. 45 C.F.R. §46.121(b)(2). Also, many institutions have taken the position that it is best to maintain consistency and review all research involving human subjects through a single process, thus avoiding the implication that research not subject to specific legal requirements for review will receive less scrutiny and, therefore, might expose subjects to greater risks by proceeding without full regard for the rights of the subjects. As more institutions move toward this position, it is possible that it may become recognized as the standard of care, so a court, hearing a case involving an institution's responsibility for research with which it had some connection, could find that all research must be reviewed through institutional processes. If such a position were adopted in determining the adequacy of review, the court might look to the requirements of the DHEW and state agencies to find evidence of the standard. We recommend reviewing all research and applying the same standards to all research, regardless of the source of funding. (However, later in this chapter we discuss the possibility of the need for a separate standard for studies that require some deception or nondisclosure.)

It is clear that all research conducted on the premises of the institution falls within the jurisdiction of the board. It is far more difficult to delineate jurisdiction over off-premises research. Use of the records of the institution clearly should be covered. Funding through the institution or involvement of people connected with the

---

* The word "research" will be used in this chapter to encompass research, development, and related activities.

institution are important factors. We suggest using the criterion of whether people are acting in connection with their responsibilities or relationships to the institution. One indication of such a connection is the use of the name of the institution in any presentation or publication concerning the research. This includes the use of the name as an address or to identify the investigator or author. We realize that, in some circumstances, it can be difficult to determine in what capacity a person is acting at a particular time. We suggest that where there is doubt the research should be reviewed. Some institutions might desire to avoid these additional complications by establishing a policy of reviewing all research that faculty, medical staff members, students, or employees are conducting. This could lead to hardships for persons who are connected with the institution part-time or who engage in research unrelated to the institution during their off-hours or vacations. For example, although it is clear that any research that a student is conducting as part of his degree requirements or for compensation through the institution should be reviewed by the board, it is less clear that the institution need or should review research activity engaged in by a student working part-time at another institution. The use of "responsibilities and relationships" could require the institution to delineate more clearly the responsibilities of its faculty, medical staff members, students, and employees, while recognizing the limits of its authority over such persons when they are conducting activities under the auspices of other institutions.

An institution might choose to adopt a policy of only reviewing the research that it is legally required to review or a policy of applying a less strict standard to research of another category. Both positions invite possible risks of future legal difficulties that cannot be clearly assessed at this time.

In the draft jurisdictional statement that follows this paragraph, "approved by the board" is used to cover two different types of board decisions: (1) a board finding that there are no subjects at risk and, thus, that the board need not review the study further; and (2) a board finding that there are subjects at risk, followed by review and approval of the study. The determination of whether there are subjects at risk is discussed in Chapter 2. The board, not the investigator, must determine whether there are subjects at risk. Thus, it is necessary for all studies involving human subjects to be submitted to the board.

Jurisdiction of the Board

All research, development, and related activities that involve human subjects and that are connected with the [Institution] must be approved by the [Board] *before* human subjects may be involved. All such research, development, and related activities that are conducted on the premises of the [Institution] are connected with the [Institution]. In addition, such research, development, and related activities conducted at sites other than the premises of the [Institution] are connected with the [Institution] if they (1) are funded through the [Institution]; or (2) are conducted by faculty, medical staff members, students, or employees of the [Institution] who are acting in connection with their responsibilities or relationships to the [Institution] or who intend to use the name of the [Institution] in any report of the activity; or (3) involve the records of the [Institution]; or (4) involve the use of the [Institution's] records, faculty, medical staff members, students, or employees to identify and/or contact its current clients, patients, or students to be subjects. For the purposes of this paragraph, a [Board] finding that there are no subjects at risk constitutes approval by the [Board].

PROTOCOL SUBMISSION

It is the responsibility of the investigator to prepare a protocol, including a consent form, that complies with the institution's "Guidelines for Preparation of Protocols" and to sign it. We recommend that each institution adopt a policy of requiring review of protocols at the department level prior to their submission to the board.   Such prior review is not required or even suggested by current federal regulations.

One purpose of prior review is to afford the person responsible for the regular treatment of the subjects or for the performance of the investigator an opportunity to learn what is being proposed. This includes informing not only the chairman of the department of a hospital about activities that will affect patients for whom he has responsibility but also includes, for example, informing the chairman of the department of a university as to the activities of faculty for whom he has administrative responsibility and the activities of students, both as investigators and subjects. Of course, this can be accomplished merely by requiring a signature without any ex-

pectation of substantive review. Many department level administrators are unwilling to conduct any substantive review. We suggest
that if substantive review is not required that, at least, the department head sign the protocol to indicate that he has had access to the
information.

The other purpose of prior review is to draw upon the expertise of
the department, which may exceed the expertise of the board on
several issues, particularly regarding the importance of the knowledge sought. A department level determination on the question of
the importance of the knowledge sought should be seriously considered by the board. Also, at the department level there should be more
familiarity with the proper design of research in its area, as well as
with the risks involved. It is often more difficult for the board to
require revision of a study design to assure that valid data are
acquired than to increase the protection of the subjects. A requirement that a study design be modified may be accepted more readily if
it emanates from departmental review or is based on departmental
comments. Responsibility for assessing the quality of research should
not be solely on the board. The board cannot avoid some responsibility because the assessment is an integral part of balancing risks
and benefits. However, the responsibility should be spread more
broadly through the institution. This policy should also reduce the
number of incomplete protocols that the chairman of the board must
scan.

In the draft procedure for protocol submission that follows this
paragraph, "department" and "chairman of the department" appear
in brackets because institutions have different organizational structures and use other titles. Blank spaces were left within brackets
because of the wide variety of possible institutional procedures
concerning some types of proposals. Each institution adopting the
policy of department level review should adopt an allocation of
responsibility, which will accomplish the goals outlined above, and
substitute the appropriate titles in the brackets.

Procedure for Protocol Submission

It is the responsibility of the investigator to prepare a protocol,
including a consent form, that complies with the [Institution]
"Guidelines for Preparation of Protocols" and to sign it. The
protocol must then be submitted to the [Chairman of the Depart-
ment] in which the research will be conducted. Research that only

involves review of records shall be submitted to [   ]. A protocol for research that will not be conducted on the premises of the [Institution] should be submitted to the [Chairman of the Department] with which principal investigator is associated. If the principal investigator is not associated with a [Department], then the protocol should be submitted to [   ].

It is the responsibility of the person designated above or his delegate to receive the protocol and to determine that the protocol is complete and that the study is designed to generate useful information. Of course, to accomplish this, changes might have to be made in the protocol. When satisfied with the protocol, the designated person should sign it. The investigator must then submit the signed protocol, with the specified number of copies, to the [Chairman of the Board].

DETERMINATIONS CONCERNING RISK-BENEFIT, RIGHTS, AND CONSENT

The first step of board review is to determine whether or not the subjects are "at risk." 45 C.F.R. §46.102(b). "Subject at risk" is defined as

> any individual who may be exposed to the possibility of injury, including physical, psychological, or social injury, as a consequence of participation as a subject in any research, development, or related activity which departs from the application of those established and accepted methods necessary to meet his needs, or which increases the ordinary risks of daily life, including the recognized risks inherent in a chosen occupation or field of service. 45 C.F.R. §46.103(b).

Since risk is so broadly defined, the only studies that will not put subjects at risk will be those seeking socially neutral information through methods of data gathering that do not increase the risk of physical or psychosocial injury above the risk that the subject would encounter if he were not participating in the study. Adding a new risk increases the total risk, even if the new risk is smaller than other risks the subject normally encounters. Socially neutral means that no social stigma would be attached to the subject, by the subject's peers or by the community at large, if the information were known widely.

If the board concludes that there are subjects at risk, it must make three additional determinations:

(1) "the risks to the subject are so outweighed by the sum of the benefit to the subject and the importance of the knowledge to be gained as to warrant a decision to allow the subject to accept these risks;"

(2) "the rights and welfare of any subjects will be adequately protected;" and

(3) "legally effective informed consent will be obtained by adequate and appropriate means." 45 C.F.R. §46.102(b).

When each of these determinations is made, the board can approve the research. Board approval is not guaranteed because the board must also take into account the acceptability of proposals in terms of "organizational commitments and regulations, applicable law, standards of professional conduct and practice, and community attitudes." 45 C.F.R. §46.106(b)(1). Many professions have adopted codes or statements of policy, and many states have enacted laws that affect various aspects of research. (See Chapter 5.) Many racial, socioeconomic, and geographic communities have expressed attitudes toward various approaches to research and types of research. Thus, the board in taking account of such matters might decline to approve a study, although the three above determinations have been favorable to the study.

From time to time the DHEW promulgates specific prohibitions of certain research areas and specific requirements concerning precautions for the rights and welfare of subjects. The board must see that such regulations are followed, at least when federal funds are sought to support the research. An example of a specific prohibition is the ban (which was lifted in 1975) on all federally funded fetal research not for the purpose of preserving the life of the fetus. That ban replaced with specific regulations concerning fetuses, *in vitro* fertilization, pregnant women, and women who could become pregnant. Specific additional responsibilities concerning such studies were specified. 45 C.F.R. §§46.102(c) and 46.205. These will be included in the discussion of voluntariness later in this chapter.

To make the first three determinations the board should examine seven factors:

(1) the knowledge to be gained from the study,

(2) prior experimental and clinical findings,

(3) potential benefits to the subjects,

(4) potential risks and procedures to minimize them,

(5) confidentiality procedures,

(6) the consent process, and
(7) the proposed subject population.

Knowledge

The importance of the knowledge to be gained from the study must be assessed. There is no formula for determining importance; it is a determination affected by individual training, experience, and understanding of societal values. The composition of the board should be designed to provide a broad perspective and to introduce some objectivity into all its determinations, including the determination of importance. Clearly, that decision is not to be limited to applied research leading to the prevention and treatment of illness; an evaluation to determine importance based on a longer time perspective is also appropriate. Thus, basic research that can lead to an understanding of how the human being functions, biologically and socially, can be important.

The adequacy of the study design to generate the projected information must be evaluated. It is unlikely that a poorly designed study could generate knowledge of sufficient importance to outweigh risks to the subjects. If your institution adopts departmental review, such review should reduce the number of inadequately designed studies submitted to the board; but the board still has the responsibility to exercise independent judgment.

A study does not have to be a double-blind, controlled study leading to quantified results that will be computer analyzed to be judged adequately designed. Although some studies might have to be so designed, in some circumstances even subjective and descriptive studies can be appropriate. The question for the board is whether the knowledge that can be gained from the proposed study is of sufficient importance.

Prior Findings

Prior experimental and clinical studies must be examined to determine the necessity and timeliness of using human subjects. If there are animal models for the phenomena being studied, prior animal studies that indicate that it is appropriate to conduct studies with humans must have been conducted. When studies involve substantial risks, consideration should be given to whether other human studies with lesser risks could be designed to yield the same information. Another issue is whether other human studies with lesser risks could be conducted first, which could provide results that would enable the investigator to modify his proposed study to reduce substantially the risks now evident.

Some studies are duplications of prior or concurrent ones. Such studies can be necessary for verification or to assemble a study population large enough to provide statistical significance. The nature of the study and the results of prior duplicate studies all enter into the decision concerning whether the additional information or benefits to the subjects outweigh the risks of involving an additional subject population.

If it is proposed to study a special population, which either cannot consent or whose consent might be questioned, then the timeliness of their involvement must be examined. There should be prior studies on a competent adult noninstitutionalized population whenever the phenomena to be studied can be studied in such a population. Prior studies should also be examined to help determine the magnitude and reliability of risk and benefit projections.

Benefits

Potential benefits to the subjects must be examined and assessed. Those potential benefits to controls and those to the other subjects are often different. Thus, it is usually necessary to consider separately the benefits to each subject group being subjected to a different treatment. (Similarly, each group may face different risks, so risks and benefits for each group will have to be balanced individually.) Many studies will have no benefits to the subjects, or some might be asserted that are not sufficiently evident for the board to consider them in its weighing process.

Delineation of what constitutes a benefit for the purposes of comparing risks and benefits is a difficult task. The line between benefits and inducements is not clear. Although the subject may feel benefited by receiving compensation for participation, this has not been considered a sufficient benefit to include in the comparing of risks and benefits. But a potential therapeutic benefit might be the greatest inducement to participation and still be a benefit for purposes of the comparison.

Risks

The magnitude of potential risks, discomforts, and inconveniences to the subjects, including controls, must be considered. The subject with whom the investigator has direct contact might not be the only subject at risk. For example, when venereal disease or contraception is involved, the sexual partner of the subject can also be a subject at risk. As the degree of risk increases, greater care must be taken to minimize the occurrence of risks. This is important both for the risk-benefit determination and for protecting the welfare of the subjects. The criteria for exclusion from the study population, the adequacy of the monitoring of crucial signs, the selection of mandatory termination threshholds, and the precautions for dealing with materialized risks must all be examined.

In discussing the comments on the original proposed regulations, it was noted that it was "also important that the committee determine that the subject will receive adequate protection against known risks." 39 Federal Register 18914, Comment B (May 30, 1974). Although this thought is not so stated in the regulations, it may be taken as an indication of what is necessary to protect adequately the welfare of the subjects. 45 C.F.R. §46.102(b)(2).

Confidentiality

Procedures to insure confidentiality and to obtain consent to disclosure of information gained through the study must include at least three aspects. First, existing confidential relationships must be respected. Thus, if names of potential subjects are obtained from a physician or an agency staff member, the physician or regular staff contact must first have approached each person and determined his willingness to discuss participation in the study with the investigator and his staff. Second, the adequacy of the procedure to provide confidentiality of the information generated by the study and of the identity of subjects must be sound. Consent must be obtained before furnishing information to organizations and to individuals other than the study staff. Third, special attention should be paid to audio or visual recordings of the subject because of a greater potential for violations of the subject's right to privacy. That such recordings will be made should be disclosed to the subject, regardless of the intended use. The subject should be told when the recordings will be destroyed. Provisions for maintaining their confidentiality should be assessed. Assurances that the recordings will be destroyed at the indicated time should be obtained. Consent of the subject should be obtained for any long-term retention of the recordings and for any showing or playing of the recordings, including such use for educational purposes, to persons other than those conducting the study.

The DHEW regulations specifically require confidentiality of any data which can be identified with the subject. 45 C.F.R. §46.119. In addition, adequate protection of the rights of the subject requires the protection of confidentiality. The adequacy of the protection can also influence the risk assessment.

Consent

The consent process must be examined to determine that it is "adequate and appropriate" to obtain "legally effective informed consent." Current DHEW regulations define "informed consent" to mean

> ... knowing consent of an individual or his legally authorized representative, so situated as to be able to exercise free power of choice without undue inducement or any element of force, fraud, deceit, duress, or other form of constraint or coercion. The basic elements of information necessary to such consent include;
> (1) a fair explanation of the procedures to be followed, and their purposes, including identification of any procedures which are experimental;
> (2) a description of any attendant discomforts and risks reasonably to be expected;
> (3) a description of any benefits reasonably to be expected;
> (4) a disclosure of any appropriate alternative procedures that might be advantageous for the subject;
> (5) an offer to answer any inquiries concerning the procedures; and
> (6) an instruction that the person is free to withdraw his consent and to discontinue participation at any time without prejudice to the subject. 45 C.F.R. §46.103(c)

There are three aspects to a "legally effective informed consent:" (1) the person consenting must be competent to consent, (2) adequate information must be presented, and (3) the consent must be voluntary. "Voluntary" is used here to mean that the person consenting is "so situated as to be able to exercise free power of choice without undue inducement or any element of force, fraud, deceit, duress, or other form of constraint or coercion." The board has one additional concern with the consent process; the process must be adequately documented.

COMPETENCY

Most research involves adult subjects of normal intelligence. Thus, there will be no question about the competency of the subjects to consent for themselves. The investigator will be expected to screen out subjects who are not competent to consent, unless he has obtained the approval of the board to use subjects who are not competent. In some cases it may be necessary to provide for additional precautions to assist the investigator to accomplish the screening.

Whenever a question concerning the competency of the study population to consent for themselves arises, the following analysis will prove useful. Competency has two aspects: legal capacity and mental capacity (ability to understand). To give legally effective consent, a person must have both legal and mental capacity to consent.

Legal Capacity. Three groups of people present questions of legal capacity to consent: children, persons adjudicated incompetent, and legal representatives. Persons who are legally incompetent cannot give effective consent regardless of their actual mental capacity.

Children under the age of majority in each state are not legally competent to authorize their own participation in research. There can be one exception to this rule. In some states, children who satisfy the requirements of the minor consent law might be deemed legally competent to consent to research that offers them potentially therapeutic treatment for a condition that they have for which there is no effective therapy. The institution's attorney should be consulted to determine the age of majority and the effects of any minor consent law or other laws in your state.

When the child is not legally competent to consent, the informed consent of the parent of guardian must be obtained. There are limits on the types of studies to which parents or guardians can consent. There is controversy concerning which risks a child may be exposed to by a parent. Some research might constitute child abuse, so the parent's consent is not only ineffective but also criminal. There is a legal action pending in California in which a former member of an institutional review board is challenging the right of the board to approve studies involving normal children. He is also challenging the right of the parents to consent to such studies. *Nielsen v. Board of Regents of California*, Docket No. 665-049 (Cal.Super.Ct., San Francisco Co.).

The DHEW has suggested that the consent of both parents be required, "except where the identity or whereabouts of either cannot be ascertained or either has been adjudicated mentally incompetent." 38 *Federal Register* 31742, §III.D.1, 31746, §46.27(c)(November 16, 1973). This has not been promulgated as a rule. However, an institution might consider requiring the consent of both parents, except when such special circumstances exist.

At the same time, the DHEW has suggested that the consent of all children who have attained the age of seven should be obtained to give them an opportunity to refuse to participate. §III.D.2, §46.27(e). The reason for this position is that the parent's role should be protective rather than coercive. Although your institution might desire to select a different age, we suggest that children who are capable of some understanding should be given an opportunity to refuse to participate. The best way to demonstrate that the child has been given an opportunity to refuse is to obtain the child's written consent. Exceptions might reasonably be made for research involving therapeutic or preventive aspects. For example, it may be reasonable not to permit a child's fear of injections to overcome a parent's desire that the child take part in field trials of a vaccine for a disease (such as polio) which constitutes a substantial natural challenge to children.

In formulating the institution's policy concerning consent of children, the statutes of the state should be examined. Some states require the consent of some or all children. For example, a recent Louisiana statute requires the consent of the subject, apparently making all consent by legal representatives alone ineffective; no exceptions are provided. La. Stat. Ann. tit. 14, §87.2 (1974).

Although prior findings can have limited predictive value if the proposed study population is significantly different from prior study populations, sometimes a countervailing rationale is present for using a population of competent adults before conducting a study on a population with restricted capacity. For instance, prior studies on adults are considered necessary before any study can involve children, unless the phenomena being studied are unique to children. Adult studies are required so that children are exposed to as well-defined a risk as possible. The potential benefit to the subject will depend on the subject's prior condition and prospects. Often there are quite different risks to some populations than to others. Children face much different risks from certain exposures than do adults.

Individuals who have been adjudicated incompetent to care for their persons (as distinguished from incompetent to manage their property) are not legally competent to authorize their own participation as subjects in research. The informed consent of the guardian over the person of the subject must be obtained. The purpose of guardianship imposes limits on the amount of risk to which a person under guardianship may be exposed. The institution's attorney should be consulted to determine the limits in your state and the circumstances for which approval of a court may be necessary.

The DHEW has proposed that, in addition to the consent of the guardian, the assent of institutionalized mentally infirm persons be required whenever they have "sufficient mental capacity to understand what is proposed and to express an opinion as to [their] participation." 39 *Federal Register* 30656, §46.504(c) (August 23, 1974). The refusal of such a person to participate in a study should not be construed to indicate a lack of mental capacity to understand. The determination should be based on other grounds. We suggest that the policy proposed by the DHEW be followed and further extended to the noninstitutionalized.

One common misconception should be clarified here; institutionalization of a person, even pursuant to a court order, does not necessarily imply that the person has been adjudicated incompetent.

In the case of a child or a person who has been adjudicated incompetent, the legal representative is ordinarily the parent or guardian designated by the court. In the case of a person who is mentally incompetent, but not adjudicated incompetent, it is not clear who is the legal representative. The DHEW has left determination of who is the legal representative to state law. The consent of the nearest relative to necessary diagnostic and therapeutic procedures is widely recognized as ordinarily effective to avoid liability on the informed consent theory. However, this practice does not necessarily imply that such relatives are the legal representatives for the purpose of consenting to participation in research. The institution's lawyer should be consulted concerning how to determine who is the legal representative in your state under various circumstances.

There are limits to the nature of the research to which a legal representative is legally competent to consent, but these limits are not well established. This is one issue that involves particular complexity in reviewing research with special populations. The board must decide whether the proposed research is of the type to which a legal representative can consent. As the extent of potential risks to the subject approach potential benefits, the effectiveness of the consent of the legal representative becomes more suspect. This is a murky area in both law and ethics. As a result, the use of additional procedural precautions is suggested when the subject population includes members of special populations whose capacity to consent is questionable.

One of the few contexts in which the limits of guardians' powers have been addressed by the courts is in cases involving parents seeking court rulings concerning their power to authorize kidney donations by their minor or incompetent children. These cases indicate that there are limits to the risks to which parents may expose their children. Therefore, the institution's legal counsel should be consulted in developing the institution's policies in this area because state laws and court decisions vary with respect to what constitutes child abuse, the duties and responsibilities of guardians, and other relevant matters.

One aspect of the legal capacity of the legal representative is clear: if the potential subject is legally and mentally competent to consent, then there is no legal representative with the capacity to consent for the subject.

Mental Capacity. The question of mental capacity concerns the subject's actual capacity to comprehend the necessary information and to reach a decision based on that information. A person who has not been declared legally incompetent is presumed to have the mental capacity to consent, until shown to be otherwise. Persons who are senile, are of extremely low intelligence, are psychotic, or have temporarily diminished capacity, all can present questions concerning whether they have sufficient mental capacity to consent. Whenever the board determines that the study population is likely to contain persons whose mental capacity may be questioned, it should require an independent assessment of mental capacity and any other steps necessary to assure that legally effective informed consent is obtained.

The DHEW has proposed requiring the assent of some of the institutionalized mentally infirm. (See the previous section on Legal Capacity.) We suggest that this policy be extended to the noninstitutionalized. Applying this policy, if it is determined that a potential subject lacks sufficient mental capacity to give effective consent for himself but has sufficient capacity to understand what is proposed and to express an opinion as to his participation, then his consent as well as the consent of his legal representative would be obtained. We suggest that whenever there is doubt whether the potential subject has the capacity to understand and to express an opinion, that the doubt be resolved in favor of requiring the person's assent. This should help minimize the misuse of the determination of mental incapacity to reduce a person's control over his own life and body. In its effort to find a legal representataive to assure legally effective consent in questionable cases, the board should not overlook its parallel duty to assure that the subject is as informed and as involved as possible in the decision-making process.

The board should be particularly sensitive to the possibility that people can have temporarily diminished capacity due to such influences as medication, fatigue, shock, and pain, especially labor pain. Reversible coma is the extreme case. It is our position that few situations exist where the board can approve reliance on the consent of a legal representative to the participation of a person with temporarily diminished capacity. While standard therapy can be given under these circumstances, pursuant to either the emergency doctrine or the consent of a legal representative, it is questionable whether research can be conducted. The Board should require that consent be obtained before the capacity of the person is reduced, whenever possible. If this is not possible, as in the case where those who suffer from the condition to be studied cannot be identified beforehand, the board should require postponement of the study until capacity is restored. If the potential subjects are not identifiable in advance and the condition being studied only exists during the period of diminished capacity, then the board should not approve the study unless it either has low risks or offers the promise of considerably more effective therapy. If those conditions obtain, then the consent of the legal representative should be secured.

If the policy outlined in the preceding paragraph were adopted, it would result in the prohibition of nontherapeutic research concerning conditions that result in temporarily diminished capacity whenever the research involves substantial risks and the consent of the subject cannot be obtained before the onset of diminished capacity. An example of such research would be a study, with more than minimal risk, of some characteristic of a person immediately after a myocardial infarction.

Research involving a woman in labor will also have to satisfy the DHEW regulations concerning research with pregnant women. 45 C.F.R. §§46.201-46.208.

INFORMATION

The DHEW regulations require the following elements of information:
(1) a fair explanation of the procedures to be followed, and their

purposes, including identification of any procedures which are experimental;

(2) a description of any attendant discomforts and risks reasonably to be expected;

(3) a description of any benefits reasonably to be expected;

(4) a disclosure of any appropriate alternative procedures that might be advantageous for the subject;

(5) an offer to answer any inquiries concerning the procedures; and

(6) an instruction that the person is free to withdraw his consent and to discontinue participation in the project or activity at any time without prejudice to the subject. 45 C.F.R. §46.103(c).

Your institution may decide to require additional elements of information. In Chapter 2, we suggested the following additional elements:

(1) a statement of the general purpose of the study;

(2) an invitation to participate;

(3) an explanation of why the subject was selected;

(4) a promise of confidentiality and a description of any disclosures that are planned;

(5) a description of any compensation the subject will receive for participation;

(6) a description of any additional costs the subject will incur; and

(7) a notification to the subject that he may decide not to participate without prejudice.

We also suggested a standard concluding paragraph that should be required whenever a full written consent form is used. The written consent part of the "Guidelines for the Preparation of Protocols" developed by your institution should be used by the board to determine whether all required information has been included.

Whichever elements your institution chooses to require, it is the responsibility of the board to determine that all are treated in the consent form, unless your institution adopts a policy of permitting some deception studies. If deception studies are permitted and the board is reviewing a deception study, then its responsibility shifts from determining whether there is full disclosure to determining whether the nondisclosure falls within your institution's policy. (See the discussion of covert and deception studies later in this chapter.)

All the information in the consent form must be presented in language that the subject can reasonably be expected to understand. It is the board's responsibility to determine that technical language, which the subject might not understand, either is removed from the consent form or is defined, unless the subject population is technically trained. If the subject does not understand or read English, we suggest that the board require the investigator to provide a translated version of the consent form and a person capable of communicating with the subject in his native language. When a patient does not understand English, most courts, in the therapeutic context, have been satisfied by the presence of an interpreter. We suggest the translated consent form in addition to the interpreter because it provides some assurance of the quality of the communication and is likely to have evidentiary value superior to that of a form in English.

The question of the level of mastery of the information by the subject that is required remains after the question of the adequacy of the information presented is resolved. An offer or presentation of information in oral or written form might be rejected, or the subject can hear or read the information but not comprehend it or admit that he was unable to understand it. Whether the board should require that the investigator establish for each subject either that a particular level of understanding or knowledge concerning participation in the study was attained or that the subject rejected an offer of information in conformity with the institution's policy is a matter for decision within the institution. Studies of the question of a subject's understanding of the research suggest that a considerable gap exists between the information provided to, and that comprehended by, consenting subjects. When substantial risks are present or when the risks outweigh the benefits to the subjects, concern about the appropriateness of involving subjects who reject proffered information or whose comprehension of information is doubtful is heightened.

VOLUNTARINESS

The person consenting must be "so situated as to be able to exercise free power of choice without undue inducement or any element of force, fraud, deceit, duress, or other form of constraint or coercion." 45 C.F.R. §46.103(c). The board should consider at least five possible sources of interference with the free power of choice: (1) the language of the disclosure of information; (2) relationships between the investigator or other persons and the subject; (3) inducements or compensation; (4) the setting in which consent will be obtained; and (5) the time when the consent will be obtained. Not all studies raise all these issues, yet some present other possible interferences.

It is virtually impossible to determine directly whether a decision is based on the "free power of choice." Thus, it must be defined by the absence of unacceptable influences and interferences, which is the approach that the DHEW regulations take. Thus, consent is deemed voluntary when there are none of the identifiable unacceptable influences or interferences at work. As long as the proscribed influences and interferences are not present, an investigator can actively solicit participation of a person as a subject in his research.

It is common for a patient either to feel a duty to a treating physician to repay a deeply felt debt of gratitude or to feel it necessary to cooperate with the treating physician to retain his good will. Physician-investigators should be alert to these feelings and avoid intentionally or inadvertently taking advantage of them. In some cases it might be necessary for the board to designate others to approach the patients.

The line between reasonable compensation and undue inducement is a matter of judgment. It depends on the economic situation of the intended study population. Reasonable compensation for time and expenses is usually appropriate. If the study involves several distinct periods of participation, it is difficult to justify a large part of the compensation being conditioned on participation in all periods; this is an inducement to complete the study. The more acceptable approach is to prorate the total payment over the periods and then pay the subject for the periods in which he or she participates. The board should review any payment schedule. The determination of whether money payment in an undue inducement depends on the income of the potential subjects. Prisoners and other institutionalized persons might find any payment particularly attractive because of the few alternative ways to obtain money, favorable treatment, or other satisfactions.

Money is not the only payment that must be scrutinized; academic credit, better grades, and special privileges for the institutionalized are just a few other possible forms of payment.

Special precautions are often necessary when groups other than competent, noninstitutionalized adults are the subject population. These precautions are designed both to protect potential subjects who are less able to protect themselves and to substantiate the obtaining of informed consent in case there are later questions. (Some possible precautions are discussed at the end of Chapter 2.)

The relationships of institutionalized persons to physicians, psychiatrists, teachers, and other officials can make it difficult for them to decline to participate in a study conducted or sponsored by such officials. The setting, and the whole institutional atmosphere itself, can discourage the independent thought that is necessary to make a considered decision.

Some settings and times are more conducive to the exercise of the power of choice than others. In one case, consent for a study of delivery was obtained in the labor room after labor began. Volunteers have been sought in the presence of large groups where peer pressures are quite strong. Usually such problems will not be present, and the good judgment of the investigator can be trusted, but occasionally the board might have to negotiate requirements concerning time and place of consent before it can approve the study.

When research involves fetuses, pregnant women, or human *in vitro* fertilization, additional protections are required by the DHEW. 45 C.F.R. §§46.201-46.211. Federal level ethical advisory boards are to be established by the DHEW to pass on such studies. The institutional review boards are given added duties. The board must examine the manner in which potential subjects are selected and must provide for monitoring of the actual consent process. §46.205(a)(2). In addition, the board must determine that appropriate studies on animals and nonpregnant persons have been completed, that the risk to the fetus is minimized, that conflicts of interest in choosing pregnancy termination technique and in assessing viability are avoided, that the experimental technique does not introduce more than minimal risk, and that no inducements are offered to terminate pregnancies. §46.206. The mother must consent and, if available, in most circumstances, the father also must consent. §§46.207(b), 46.208(b), and 46.209(d).

In addition, it is the responsibility of the board, whenever the study could involve risk to a fetus and does not clearly fall under the above regulations, to determine that adequate steps will be taken to avoid the involvement of women who are in fact pregnant. 45 C.F.R. §46.102(c).

DOCUMENTATION

The means of documenting consent must also be examined by the board. Current federal regulations provide three ways to document consent: (1) written consent, (2) "short form" written consent, and (3) modified consent. The language of the regulations follows:

45 C.F.R. §46.110
The documentation of consent will employ one of the following three forms:
(a) Provision of a written consent document embodying all of the basic elements of informed consent. This may be read

to the subject or to his legally authorized representative, but in any event he or his legally authorized representative must be given adequate opportunity to read it. This document is to be signed by the subject or his legally authorized representative. Sample copies of the consent form as approved by the Board are to be retained in its records.

(b) Provision of a "short form" written consent document indicating that the basic elements of informed consent have been presented orally to the subject or his legally authorized representative. Written summaries of what is to be said to the patient are to be approved by the Board. The short form is to be signed by the subject or his legally authorized representative and by an auditor witness to the oral presentation and to the subject's signature. A copy of the approved summary, annotated to show any additions, is to be signed by the persons officially obtaining the consent and by the auditor witness. Sample copies of the consent form and of the summaries as approved by the Board are to be retained in its records.

(c) Modification of either of the primary procedures outlined in paragraphs (a) and (b) of this section. Granting of permission to use modified procedures imposes additional responsibility upon the Board and the institution to establish: (1) that the risk to any subject is minimal, (2) that use of either of the primary procedures for obtaining informed consent would surely invalidate objectives of considerable immediate importance, and (3) that any reasonable alternative means for attaining these objectives would be less advantageous to the subjects. The Board's reasons for permitting the use of modified procedures must be individually and specifically documented in the minutes and in reports of Board actions to the files of the institution. All such modifications should be regularly reconsidered as a function of continuing review and as required for annual review, with documentation of reaffirmation, revision, or discontinuation, as appropriate.

*   *   *

45 C.F.R. §46.109

No such informed consent, oral or written, obtained under an assurance provided pursuant to this part shall include any explanatory language through which the subject is made to waive, or to appear to waive, any of his legal rights, including any release of the organization or its agents from liability for negligence.

Although current federal regulations do not indicate a preference for the written consent document, we suggest that your institution adopt a policy of requiring it. (See the discussion in Chapter 2.) This would give the board the duty of determining that the investigator had shown that the "short form" would be advantageous to the subject or that the conditions for the modified consent were present before the board could authorize the "short form" or the modified procedure, respectively.

COVERT AND DECEPTION STUDIES

Many psychological and behavioral studies are either covert or involve elements of deception. Although some authors believe that such studies should not be permitted, others argue that, with suitable precautions, they are permissible. However, the circumstances in which such studies are viewed as permissible have decreased as psychologists and other behavioral scientists have grown more sensitive to the risks to the subjects.

The DHEW has not yet published regulations dealing specifically with psychological and social science research. If it follows the pattern of its regulation of other research, it will probably specifically permit some observation and deception studies under special precautions. However, as the regulations are now written, the status of such studies is in question. Observation studies are obviously possible under the regulations when they do not place subjects at risk. However, since psychological and social science researchers often select the most controversial aspects of behavior to study, observation studies can place subjects at the risk of social injury. Deception studies virtually always will place subjects at some risk of either psychological or social injury. Since the definition of informed consent in the regulations includes a requirement of "knowing consent . . . without . . . any element of . . . fraud [or] deceit," it is difficult to imagine deception studies that could comply. On the other hand, the modified procedure might be interpreted to apply to some observation and deception studies where there are minimal risks.

If your institution decides to permit covert and deception studies, we recommend that it adopt a separate policy and a modified procedure for such research rather than attempting to use the DHEW provision for the modified procedure. (Of course, if DHEW funding is involved, the standards of the department must be applied and met. Inquiries to the DHEW may be necessary to determine its current practice before the board conducts its review.) The nature of reactions to the performance of such studies demands that the circumstances in which they will be permitted be carefully delineated and that precautions to minimize the risks to the subjects and the exposure to liability of the investigator and the institution be required. When institutions are sued, it is becoming increasingly common for their own policies and procedures to be admitted as evidence of the standard of care to which they should be held. If an institution approved covert and deceptive studies without having a policy that clearly permitted such approval and if harm were to result from the studies, its own policies would weaken its defensive position in any resulting litigation. Carefully developed policies and procedures, which had been followed, could be useful to demonstrate the institution's concern for the rights and welfare of subjects of such studies.

Two possible approaches to providing review of such studies are (1) to establish a separate board with its own policies and procedures document or (2) to give the present board additional jurisdiction to act pursuant to either a separate policies and procedures document or a special section applying to such studies in the institution's overall policy and procedures document.

We suggest that the American Psychological Association's *Ethical Principles in the Conduct of Research with Human Participants* (1973) be consulted in developing institutional policies. Those principles are not in a form that would constitute an adequate institutional policy; but the principles, along with the examples and discussions, will help to identify problem areas and some possible safeguards. At a minimum, the following approaches should be considered:

(1) deception and nondisclosure should only be permitted when the information sought is of great importance and cannot be obtained through other means;

(2) deception and nondisclosure should be limited to only that which is necessary to gain the information of such importance;

(3) they should be employed only when the disclosure would eliminate the effect being studied, not when the disclosure would merely lead people to refuse to participate;

(4) the study design should be carefully scrutinized to determine that the information can actually be obtained;

(5) at the conclusion of the study, the study should be explained in its entirety to the subject; and

(6) at that time the subject's consent to use the information generated by the study should be obtained. If the subject does not
consent, the information concerning him should be destroyed.

These methods should help discourage investigators from using
deception merely as a recruitment device. None of the precautions
will insulate the investigator or the institution from liability for
invasion of privacy or for failing to obtain informed consent. They
should, however, contribute to minimizing the amount of exposure to
liability.

It can be tempting to view exposure to liability for deception and
observation studies as limited because the subjects do not know in
some instances that they are being studied or in others the purpose of
a study or the extent of their involvement. This view could lead to
opposing debriefing subjects because it alerts them to the fact they
were involved and, thus, might encourage them to seek legal redress.
However, the study will eventually be published; and it is possible
that it will eventually come to the attention of the subjects. The
institution and the investigator are then in a more difficult position
than they would have been if they had confronted the issue immediately.

OTHER CONCERNS OF THE BOARD

Follow-Up

It is usually important that the subjects be contacted one or more
times after their involvement in a study is otherwise completed.
Such a follow-up procedure makes it possible to detect the long-term
effects of the study. This helps to protect the subject and also can help
discover phenomena that would otherwise not be learned.

The board should assess the adequacy of the provisions for follow-
up. Often an investigator either will lose interest in the subjects as
soon as the study data is obtained and analyzed or will move to
another geographic location leaving no one with the responsibility
for follow-up. This can be a particular problem in a university
setting, where students and junior and visiting faculty are particularly transient. Where there is some doubt whether an investigator
will be available to conduct the necessary follow-up, additional
investigators should be required who will be responsible for the
follow-up.

Review

The board periodically must review each of the continuing studies it has previously approved. The DHEW regulations require review at least annually. This review sometimes becomes perfunctory. However, the board must be alert to changes in the law or the community, which might require it to revise its earlier determination concerning a particular study.

Conflicts Between Boards

Sometimes one proposal must be reviewed by more than one board within an institution or by the boards of separate institutions. A decision by one board to recommend approval of a study is not binding on any other board. Thus, the possibility of conflicting recommendations exists. If one board within an institution recommends approval of a study and another does not, the institution cannot furnish the necessary approval for DHEW funding unless the study is changed so it either can be removed from the disapproving board's jurisdiction on a legitimate basis, or approved on reconsideration by the disapproving board, because the objections have been obviated by the changes made. Where the conflicting recommendations are of boards of separate institutions, the institution whose board has recommended that the study not be approved cannot approve that study.

DUTIES AND PROCEDURES OF THE BOARD

For the board to function in an orderly and thorough fashion, it should have a set of procedures either established by the institution or adopted by the board itself. A draft of a possible procedure document follows this paragraph. It has three parts: (1) Duties of the Chairman of the Board, (2) Duties of the Primary and Secondary Reviewers, and (3) Conduct of Board Deliberations. The designation of reviewers is recommended as a method of assuring close scrutiny for each protocol. Wherever "board" appears in the following draft, substitute the term used for your institutional review board.

Duties of the Chairman of the Board

(1) All protocols submitted at least a week before the meeting shall be skimmed by the [Chairman] for completeness. Incomplete

protocols shall be returned to the investigator, along with a copy of the guidelines for protocol preparation, with the violated sections circled or otherwise indicated. Protocols that appear to be complete shall be assigned numbers sequentially as they are submitted.

(2) For each protocol the [Chairman] shall designate one [Board] member as primary reviewer and a second member as secondary reviewer. This responsibility should be spread as evenly as possible among the members over the year. However, rather than a mere rotation scheme, whenever a member is particularly qualified to note the difficulties with a given protocol, such member should be designated the primary reviewer.

(3) The [Chairman] shall promptly forward a copy of each protocol to each member of the committee.

(4) If there is no business to be conducted at the next scheduled meeting, the [Chairman] shall promptly notify the [Board] members that the meeting is cancelled.

(5) At the request of a member of the [Board] or on his own determination, the [Chairman] shall request that the investigator be present to answer questions during the meeting.

(6) The [Chairman] shall notify the [appropriate institutional officer here] and the investigator of the [Board's] determination. If the determination is not unanimous, the notification should specify the vote and the major reasons for the dissenting vote. In addition, any suggestions for changes in the protocol that the [Board] decides not to require, but which would provide increased protection to subjects, should be mentioned in the notification because the investigator might wish to implement them on his own.

Duties of the Primary and Secondary Reviewers

(1) The reviewers shall examine the protocols assigned to them in depth. They should be prepared to point out the deficiencies in the protocol and, if possible, suggest modifications to correct them.

(2) As the reviewers' schedules permit, if the protocol is unclear or raises technical or novel questions, the reviewers shall obtain clarification from the investigator and/or consult appropriate literature and/or experts.

(3) If minor modifications will correct the protocol's deficiencies (for example, changes in the wording of the consent form or specifying additional criteria for exclusion of subjects), the re-

viewers shall contact the investigator informally and determine his willingness to accept the suggested changes if the [Board] should so require. It must be made clear that the reviewers cannot speak for the entire [Board] and that acceptance of the reviewers' proposals will not guarantee [Board] approval. It is expected that, as the [Board] becomes more experienced, this procedure will eliminate most of the recurring minor deficiencies, which often lead to conditional approvals.

Conduct of Board Deliberations

(1) The primary reviewer will report on any deficiencies in the protocol and his suggested modifications. (All members shall have read the protocol to participate in [Board] deliberations.) He will also report with regard to the acceptability of the modifications to the investigator.

(2) The secondary reviewer will report on any differences he has with the primary reviewer's position.

(3) Other [Board] members will report their preliminary observations, if different from the reviewers.

(4) If there is apparent disagreement, the [Board] will discuss the protocol and possible modifications.

(5) If additional information is needed that the investigator can provide, he will be called into the room or contacted by telephone. The investigator can only be present to give information and must be excused before the [Board] resumes its deliberations.

(6) By majority vote, the [Board] will make one of the following determinations:

(a) approved, no human subjects at risk;

(b) approved, as written;

(c) approved, if specified modifications are made;

(d) cannot be approved at this time, additional information needed, specifying the information needed and who will be responsible for gathering it;

(e) cannot be approved at this time, major modifications are needed to correct specified deficiencies;

(f) cannot be approved at this time, the [Board] needs additional time to consider specified controversial or complex aspects of the protocol [and the board, in its discretion, may appoint a subcommittee to consider the issues and report back to the board]; or

(g) rejected, there is no way to gather the data that is both acceptable to the investigator and the [Board].

(7) As a matter of [Board] procedure, determination (g) will not be made at the first meeting at which a protocol is reviewed. The investigator will be given an opportunity to develop a protocol that the [Board] can approve or to decide to abandon the proposed investigation.

(8) If the study is approved, the [Board] will determine the period of approval. A study cannot be approved for a period longer than one year.

4

INSTITUTIONAL ADMINISTRATIVE RESPONSIBILITIES TO HUMAN SUBJECTS

Grants and contracts for research involving human subjects, though usually awarded because of the talent and knowledge of particular investigators, ordinarily are awarded to institutions. Thus the institutions in which such research is conducted must administer the funds and, depending on the requirements imposed by the sponsor of the research, assume a variety of responsibilities. The institutions also have obligations to the public and, particularly, to subjects whose participation is crucial to the carrying out of the research activity. This chapter is concerned with the nature and extent of the responsibilities of the institution for the aspects of research involving human subjects that relate to their protection.

The regulations of the DHEW provide a format for consideration of many of these aspects of such research; however, the discussion of the issues to which the institutional administration must direct attention is not limited to these alone.

INSTITUTIONAL RESPONSIBILITY

45 C.F.R. §46.102 Policy

(a) Safeguarding the rights and welfare of subjects at risk in activities supported under grants and contracts from

DHEW is primarily the responsibility of the institution which receives or is accountable to DHEW for the funds awarded for the support of the activity. In order to provide for the adequate discharge of this institutional responsibility, it is the policy of DHEW that no activity involving human subjects to be supported by DHEW grants or contracts shall be undertaken unless an Institutional Review Board has reviewed and approved such activity, and the institution has submitted to DHEW a certification of such review and approval, in accordance with the requirements of this part.

*   *   *

(e) No grant or contract involving human subjects at risk shall be made to an individual unless he is affiliated with or sponsored by an institution which can and does assume responsibility for the subjects involved.

45 C.F.R. §46.103 Definitions

*   *   *

(g) "Certification" means the official institutional notification to DHEW in accordance with the requirements of this part that a project or activity involving human subjects at risk has been reviewed and approved by the institution in accordance with the "approved assurance" on file at DHEW.

The foregoing provisions clearly state that the primary responsibility for protection of subjects in studies supported with DHEW funds is on the institution and that the mechanism for review of activities is the Institutional Review Board, which must grant approval. The institution must certify that review and approval by the board has taken place for each activity involving human subjects. When an application or proposal involves an investigational new drug, a specific statement regarding the thirty-day delay requirement must be included as part of the certification. (See 45 C.F.R. §46.117.)

45 C.F.R. §46.104 Submission of assurances

(a) Recipients or prospective recipients of DHEW support under a grant or contract involving subjects at risk shall provide written assurance acceptable to DHEW that they will comply with DHEW policy as set forth in this part. Each assurance shall embody a statement of compliance with DHEW requirements for initial and continuing Institutional Review Board review of the supported activities; a set of implementing guidelines, including identification of the Board and a description of its review procedures; or, in the case of special assurances concerned with single activities or projects, a report of initial findings of the Board and of its proposed continuing review procedures.

(b) Such assurance shall be executed by an individual authorized to act for the institution and to assume on behalf of the institution the obligations imposed by this part, and shall be filed in such form and manner as the Secretary may require.

45 C.F.R. §46.105 Types of assurances

(a) *General assurances.* A general assurance describes the review and implementation procedures applicable to all DHEW-supported activities conducted by an institution regardless of the number, location, or types of its components or field activities. General assurances will be required from institutions having a significant number of concurrent DHEW-supported projects or activities involving human subjects.

(b) *Special assurances.* A special assurance will, as a rule, describe those review and implementation procedures applicable to a single activity or project. A special assurance will not be solicited or accepted from an institution which has on file with DHEW an approved general assurance.

Each institution receiving grant or contract support for research involving human subjects must provide a written assurance to the DHEW regarding review and approval of supported activities by the Institutional Review Board and other information stated above. The major difference between a general and special assurance is that the former is required of "institutions having a significant number of concurrent DHEW-supported projects and activities involving human subjects," but the special assurance is furnished by the institution for a single activity or project and describes the "review and implementation procedures" for the particular activity or project.

MINIMUM REQUIREMENTS FOR GENERAL ASSURANCES

45 C.F.R. §46.106 Minimum requirements for general assurances

(a) A statement of principles which will govern the institution in the discharge of its responsibilities for protecting the rights and welfare of subjects. This may include appropriate existing codes or declarations, or statements formulated by the institution itself. It is to be understood that no such principles supersede DHEW policy or applicable law.

Statement of Principles

Many institutions engaged in research involving human subjects have adopted one or more statements of principles for the conduct of such research. Some of these statements, adopted in the past, might not be fully reflective of current institutional responsibilities. Part of the obligation of an institution's administration is periodic evaluation of the principles governing research with which it is concerned and recommendation of changes in the statement to reflect changed governmental requirements and new information.

Frequent reference in Chapters 2 and 3 is made to determinations of policy by the institution on many issues. These policy decisions must be embodied in some tangible form; and the statement of principles is the document in which many should appear. The statement of principles has a number of purposes; (1) it informs investigators of the rules that govern their research proposals and activities; (2) it provides standards to be applied by the board in the review of protocols and in the conduct of periodic review of ongoing projects; (3) it signifies to prospective subjects that there is an institutional policy for oversight of research activities; and (4) it evidences a standard that the institutional administration can apply, if charges are made by individual subjects, the media, sponsors of research, or outside organizations, that inappropriate or illegal activity in the conduct of research has occurred, to help determine the validity and substantiality of such charges. The measures to be considered when there has been an apparent or actual violation of the principles in the conduct of a research study are discussed in another part of this chapter.

A very basic issue with regard to the statement of principles concerns the selection of the proper authority to adopt it. There are several possible choices—the chief administrative officer, the governing body of the institution, or some other authority such as, in the case of a state governmental hospital, the director of the state agency or department that operates the hospital. If the statement of principles is to represent policy for the institution, the institution's governing body should adopt the statement rather than the executive. Where there is no governing body for the institution, as is often the case for certain state and local government institutions, the statement should be adopted on behalf of the institution by the governmental officer under whose departmental jurisdiction the institution is placed.

Adoption is the formal process of establishing policy. This does not preclude the involvement of administrative officers and professionals of the institution, or the board itself, from proposing content and drafting language for the statement of principles. Adoption by the governing body emphasizes that the statement represents an institutional commitment, binding on all staff and, in the case of educational institutions, students, who conduct research involving human subjects, as well as those using the facilities, records, and charts of the institution for such research. (See the jurisdiction statement for the Institutional Review Board in chapter 3.)

Institutional Review Board Composition

45 C.F.R. §46.106

*   *   *

(b) An Institutional Review Board or Board structure which will conduct initial and continuing reviews in accordance with the policy outlined in §46.102. Such Board structure or Board shall meet the following requirements:

(1) The Board must be composed of not less than five persons with varying backgrounds to assure complete and adequate review of activities commonly conducted by the institution. The Board must be sufficiently qualified through the maturity, experience, and expertise of its members and diversity of its membership to insure respect for its advice and counsel for safeguarding the rights and welfare of human subjects. In addition to possessing the professional competence necessary to review specific activities, the Board must be able to ascertain the acceptability of applications and proposals in terms of institutional commitments and regulations, applicable law, standards of professional conduct and practice, and community attitudes. The Board must therefore include persons whose concerns are in these areas.

(2) The Board members shall be identified to DHEW by name; earned degrees, if any; position or occupation; representative capacity; and by other pertinent indications of experience such as board certification, licenses, etc., sufficient to describe each member's chief anticipated contributions to Board deliberations. Any employment or other relationship between each member and the institution shall be identified,

i.e., full-time employee, part-time employee, member of governing panel or board, paid consultant, unpaid consultant. Changes in Board membership shall be reported to DHEW in such form and at such times as the Secretary may require.

(3) No member of a Board shall be involved in either the initial or continuing review of an activity in which he has a conflicting interest, except to provide information requested by the Board.

(4) No Board shall consist entirely of persons who are officers, employees, or agents, of, or are otherwise associated with the institution, apart from their membership on the Board.

(5) No Board shall consist entirely of members of a single professional group.

(6) The quorum of the Board shall be defined, but may in no event be less than a majority of the total membership duly convened to carry out the Board's responsibilities under the terms of the assurance.

The requirements in the foregoing provision regarding board composition are fairly straightforward. However, these requirements leave to the institution considerable discretion. Among the subjects to be considered are the following: (1) Shall there be one board or, as in the case of a university, several for different schools and divisions in which research involving human subjects is conducted? (2) By what process should board members be selected? (3) How many members should the board (or boards) have? (4) Should the quorum be more than a simple majority of board members? (5) What is an appropriate mix of persons associated and persons not associated with the institution in the composition of a board?

The answers to all the foregoing questions, while they contain policy elements to some extent, are essentially administrative in nature. The institution's governing body may choose to limit the range of administrative discretion that might be exercised in answering some or all these questions; but, in the case of most educational and health service provider institutions, the decisions regarding selection and composition would appear to be within the scope of institutional administration.

(1) *One Board vs. Several Boards.* The most important factor in answering this question is the volume of protocols to be reviewed. There are limits on the amount of time that can be committed to board activity by faculty, medical staff members, and others associ-

ated with the institution, because of other institutional duties. A heavy time commitment might also serve to discourage many qualified persons not associated with the institution from accepting membership on the board. As Chapter 3 makes clear, board members have responsibilities of board service beyond attending meetings; and the institution's administration should seek to avoid board membership becoming so onerous that the board's work is performed in a perfunctory way by persons other than those best qualified to make the decisions in the review and approval process. Thus, it might be advisable that a university have several boards; one board for the medical school, one for the other health professional schools, and a third with responsibility for research involving human subjects in other divisions and schools of the university. Where there is more than one board within the institution, the administration must delineate clearly the jurisdiction for each. Under no circumstances should a structure be established in which an investigator could choose one board from among different boards for submitting his protocol in the hope that review would be less searching by that one. Although the possibility exists that two different boards at an institution might reach different determinations during the review and approval of an identical protocol, with one board appearing more strict than the other, an investigator should not have the opportunity to choose his board to facilitate a favorable decision because of conflicting jurisdictional statements. Where there is more than one board, as a general rule there should not be the need for a protocol to be reviewed by more than one board unless more than one school or division of the institution relating to different boards are to be involved with the study and there is reason to believe the protection of subjects requires review by more than one board. The jurisdictional statements for the different boards should be drawn carefully to avoid unnecessary and time-consuming duplicate review by different boards of a single institution.

Volume of board activity has another dimension. The institutional administration should maintain records of the number of protocols reviewed and the number of meetings held by each board. Their records should be reviewed on a periodic basis. If the information in these records indicates that a board has extremely limited activity, its jurisdiction could be assigned to another board to eliminate an unnecessary structure. Members of a board that meets sporadically and has few protocols to review might lose interest in the review activity and devote little attention to the decisions they are called on to make.

(2) *Selection of Board Members.* In many institutions, such as universities and hospitals, a considerable degree of self-government for faculty and medical staff, respectively, has been adopted. At educational institutions students have been elected to boards, committees, etc., to participate in governance. Given the nature of an institution's obligations to the DHEW and the requirements for board member qualifications, the issue of whether and (if so) to what extent election processes can be utilized to provide board members is a serious one.

If there is no particular interest in, or desire for, the use of elective processes, the institutional administration can secure recommendations of persons qualified to serve as board members from a variety of sources within and outside the institution. In educational institutions, for example, prospective nominees can be solicited from deans, department chairmen, other academic administrators, and current board members. Additionally, faculty already involved in research as investigators are prospective candidates for service on the board; investigators can serve as long as they do not participate in review of their own activities.

At institutions where the practice has been to use the elective processes for selection of persons to meet institutional obligations regarding research, these practices can be continued. However, the processes have to be designed so only those who have qualifications necessary for board membership are eligible to be candidates. Since the regulations do not require individual competencies but focus on the qualifications of the board as a whole, the institutional administration need only intervene in a nominating process to insure that clearly unqualified individuals are not presented to the electorate. By pairing nominees with similar qualifications for a particular vacancy, or by establishing a field from which two or more candidates will be elected, elective processes can be used without great difficulty.

A mixture of election and administrative appointment can also be employed, where some members are elected and, after the election, appointments for the remaining vacancies are made to insure that the board contains the requisite competence and balance required by the regulations. However, it must be emphasized that the institution has the responsibility to see that the board is sufficiently qualified in line with the regulations. The selection process or processes used must result in fulfilling this responsibility.

(3) and (4) *Board Size and Quorum Requirements.*—The size of the board and the quorum requirements are intimately related. The regulations provide that a quorum consists of at least a majority of the

total membership of the board and that a board be composed of at least five members. Even if the recommendations for definite scheduling of Board meetings in Chapter 3 are followed, there is the danger that a board of five persons might prove too small, particularly when some board members are also investigators or may have other conflicting interests and cannot participate in deliberations and decisions concerning activities in which they have such an interest. If two members are absent from a meeting of a five-member board, approval of a protocol in which an attending board member has an interest is precluded by the quorum requirement.

Another factor to consider is the volume of board review activity. If the primary and secondary reviewer recommendations in Chapter 3 are followed, a larger number of board members will allow for wider distribution of the reviewer duties and reduce somewhat the amount of effort required of each board member. A board composed of seven or nine members would probably avoid many quorum difficulties, allow for the reviewer work to be apportioned without creating too great burdens, introduce wider expertise to board deliberations, and yet not be too large a group for effective functioning.

A technique that may be employed to reduce attendance and quorum difficulties is to appoint alternates for each board member. The individuals selected as alternates would have to possess the requisite qualifications for board membership. When a board member could not attend a particular meeting, his alternate would be notified by the chairman that his participation in that meeting was necessary. The use of alternates should eliminate any need to cancel or reschedule board meetings because of the inability of board members to attend meetings.

Whether the quorum requirement should exceed a simple majority of the board is not an easy question to answer. The quorum consisting of a simple majority, rather than a greater number, is generally considered to facilitate decision making by reducing the number of meetings at which no decision can be made. An institutional administrator might well be made uneasy when notified that the board consisting of nine members, functioning under a simple majority quorum rule, has approved a study with substantial risks by a three-to-two vote. Of course, the institutional administration is under no obligation to permit a study that the board has approved. Thus, it may exercise administrative prerogatives and decide not to allow the proposal to be forwarded to a sponsoring agency or take other negative action, unless changes are made in the study design, the study is evaluated by consultants, or other, additional procedures followed. The board's approval is only a recommendation to the institutional administration and should be recognized as such by the board, investigators, and the institutional administration. (See 45 C.F.R. §46.118, which describes the executive responsibility of the institution. Additional discussion of this provision appears later in this chapter.) At the same time, there might be reasons not to override board approval, such as avoiding the appearance that the institutional administration is too heavy-handed and intrusive.

One possible approach to avoid the situation described above and to achieve the participation of more board members in the review and approval process is to allow, or to require, the board chairman to raise the quorum requirement to two-thirds of the board membership when substantial risks to subjects are present. (Other methods that can be used in the close vote situation, which do not directly involve the quorum requirement, are to provide either that approval requires a two-thirds vote or that where the activity is approved by a one-vote margin it be subject to review and approval at a subsequent board meeting.)

(5) *Mix of Board Membership.* The DHEW regulations provide that the board not consist entirely of persons associated with the institution. This requirement is met by having one board member who is not associated with the institution; however, there may be advantages to having more than one outside member.

The evident rationale of that DHEW requirement is to provide an independent voice in the deliberations and processes of the board. Ideally, one would hope that the independent voice would be heard at all board meetings; but with only one member who is not associated with the institution there is a likelihood that schedule conflicts will result in that board member's absence from time to time. To better meet the spirit of the requirement, two such members are advisable.

The criteria for selection of board members not associated with the institution are no different from those for other members. They should be selected because of their qualifications, in terms of professional competence and ability to aid the board in meeting its responsibility to safeguard subjects. Ministers, attorneys, and physicians in private practice are among the persons who often would be qualified for board membership. With regard to selection of researchers from other institutions, two conflicting considerations are raised. On the one hand, their familiarity with research activity can be beneficial to the board's activity. On the other, there may be some concern that research ideas might be pirated by representatives of other institutions; research is now recognized as a competitive enterprise.

The institutional administration is required to identify by name and provide specified descriptive information about the members of the board to the DHEW in its general assurance. The regulations further require that changes in board membership be reported to the DHEW.

Procedures for Initial and Continuing Review

45 C.F.R. §46.106

    *   *   *

(c) Procedures which the institution will follow in its initial and continuing review of applications, proposals, and activities.

The requirement for a description of review procedures can be met by a summary of parts of Chapters 2 and 3, particularly the Guidelines for Protocol Preparation and the process for board functioning. There may be advantages in submitting copies of documents prepared by the institution to aid investigators in the preparation of protocols and board members in the fulfilling of their responsibilities, along with the summary descriptions.

Board Procedures for Advising and Reporting

45 C.F.R. §46.106

    *   *   *

(d) Procedures which the Board will follow (1) to provide advice and counsel to activity directors and investigators with regard to the Board's actions, (2) to insure prompt reporting to the Board of proposed changes in an activity and of unanticipated problems involving risk to subjects or others, and (3) to insure that any such problems, including adverse reactions to biologicals, drugs, radioisotope labelled drugs, or to medical devices, are promptly reported to DHEW.

This paragraph of the regulations calls for three sets of procedures.

(1) *Advising and Counseling Activity Directors and Investigators with Regard to the Board's Actions.* Recommended procedures for board activity are described in Chapter 3. They clearly encompass interaction by the board with investigators so material submitted to the board for its review and approval meet the standards under which

the board functions. At several places mention is made of contact by the chairman or reviewers with investigators concerning specific issues raised in regard to protocols. In addition, the Guidelines for Protocol Preparation developed at your institution can serve as a source of material to aid in the preparation of the necessary statement.

(2) *Prompt Reporting to the Board of Proposed Changes in an Activity or Unanticipated Problems Involving Risks.* Procedures that the board requires investigators to follow in informing the board need to be included in the statement. These procedures should indicate the threshholds that require informing the board by example.

(3) *Prompt Reporting to the DHEW.* The statement should indicate that the chairman of the board or the administrator assigned to maintain regular contact with the board inform the DHEW of problems as soon as they have been assessed by the board.

Institutional Procedures to Maintain an Active and Effective Board

45 C.F.R. §46.106

*   *   *

(e) Procedures which the institution will follow to maintain an active and effective Board and to implement its recommendations.

This requirement makes clear that under the DHEW regulations the institutional administration has a continuing responsibility for board activity. At this juncture it becomes apparent that the chief executive officer of the institution must assign an institutional administrator to maintain regular contact with the board. The procedures to be followed by the assigned administrator should include the following:

(1) review of the board's agenda for each of its meetings to determine whether, because of the nature of a particular study, his presence on behalf of the administration is necessary;

(2) review of the minutes of all board meetings;

(3) maintaining a record of board member attendance;

(4) meeting periodically with the board chairman, or the board itself, to discuss possible changes in the statement of principles adopted by the institution's governing body, in the guideline document for protocol preparation, and other procedural documents affecting the activities of the board;

(5) furnishing to the board references to, or copies of, journal articles and other information relating to research review issues and processes, such as information provided by the institution's legal counsel regarding new legal developments;

(6) reporting to the board promptly any inquiries about, or changes concerning, research that is being conducted, which have been received by the institution; and

(7) organizing periodic seminars or instructional programs for investigators at which the statement of principles and guideline documents are explained.

At institutions where there is more than one board to carry out the Institutional Review Board functions, it may be advantageous to create an institutional committee to link the various boards and the institutional administration. The committee could be composed of the chairmen of the boards plus additional members drawn from the institutional administration and staff. The functions of the committee would be to assure consistency in approach in the conduct of review by the boards, to provide a forum for discussion of problems, and to recommend changes in procedures followed and standards used by the boards. The committee should not be viewed as supplanting the administrator assigned to maintain contact with the board or boards, but as an assistance in the performance of his functions.

MINIMUM REQUIREMENTS FOR SPECIAL ASSURANCES

45 C.F.R. §46.107 Minimum requirements for special assurances

Special assurances shall be submitted in such form and manner as the Secretary may require. An acceptable special assurance shall:

(a) Identify the specific grant or contract involved by its full title; and by the name of the activity or project director, principal investigator, fellow, or other person immediately responsible for the conduct of the activity.

(b) Include a statement, executed by an appropriate institutional official, indicating that the institution has established an Institutional Review Board satisfying the requirements of §46.106(b).

(c) Describe the makeup of the Board and the training, experience, and background of its members, as required by §46.106(b)(2).

(d) Describe in general terms the risks to subjects that the Board recognizes as inherent in the activity, and justify its decision that these risks are so outweighed by the sum of the benefit to the subject and the importance of the knowledge to be gained as to warrant the Board's decision to permit the subject to accept these risks.

(e) Describe the informed consent procedures to be used and attach documentation as required by §46.110.

(f) Describe procedures which the Board will follow to insure prompt reporting to the Board of proposed changes in the activity and of any unanticipated problems, involving risks to subjects or others and to insure that any such problems, including adverse reactions to biologicals, drugs, radioisotope labelled drugs, or to medical devices are promptly reported to DHEW.

(g) Indicate at what time intervals the Board will meet to provide for continuing review. Such review must occur no less than annually.

(h) Be signed by the individual members of the Board and be endorsed by an appropriate institutional official.

The requirements for special assurances are less detailed and complex than those for general assurances. A special assurance must be submitted for each specific grant or contract. It must indicate that an Institutional Review Board has approved the activity, the qualifications of the board members, the nature of the risk and benefit assessment made by the board, the informed consent procedures (with documentation information), and the reporting and continuing review procedures the board will follow. It must be signed by the individual board members and endorsed by an appropriate institutional official.

It is evident that this section requires that the institution, in regard to Institutional Review Board composition and function, follow essentially the same requirements that apply to institutions with general assurances. An institution anticipating any volume of research activity would probably be well advised to submit a general assurance for approval, rather than submit individual special assurances.

It should be noted that the Secretary of HEW may permit submission of a special assurance containing only the identification of the grant or contract and a statement that an Institutional Review Board has been established with the proposal or application. However, the remaining information for a special assurance must be supplied before processing of the application or proposal is completed by the DHEW. (See 45 C.F.R. §46.112.)

COOPERATIVE ACTIVITIES

45 C.F.R. §46.116 Cooperative activities
Cooperative activities are those which involve institutions in addition to the grantee or prime contractor (such as a contractor under a grantee or a subcontractor under a prime contractor). If, in such instances, the grantee or prime contractor obtains access to all or some of the subjects involved through one or more cooperating institutions, the basic DHEW policy applies and the grantee or prime contractor remains responsible for safeguarding the rights and welfare of the subjects.

(a) *Institution with approved general assurance.* Initial and continuing review by the institution may be carried out by one or a combination of procedures:

(1) Cooperating institution with approved general assurance. When the cooperating institution has on file with DHEW an approved general assurance, the grantee or contractor may, in addition to its own review, request the cooperating institution to conduct an independent review and to report its recommendations on those aspects of the activity that concern individuals for whom the cooperating institution has responsibility under its own assurance to the grantee's or contractor's Institutional Review Board. The grantee or contractor may, at its discretion, concur with or further restrict the recommendations of the cooperating institution. It is the responsibility of the grantee or contractor to maintain communication with the Boards of the cooperating institution. However, the cooperating institution shall promptly notify the grantee or contracting institution whenever the cooperating institution finds the conduct of the project or activity within its purview unsatisfactory.

(2) Cooperating institution with no approved general assurance. When the cooperating institution does not have an approved general assurance on file with DHEW, the DHEW

may require the submission of a general or special assurance which, if approved, will permit the grantee or contractor to follow the procedure outlined in the preceding subparagraph.

(3) Interinstitutional joint review. The grantee or contracting institution may wish to develop an agreement with cooperating institutions to provide for an Institutional Review Board with representatives from cooperating institutions. Representatives of cooperating institutions may be appointed as ad hoc members of the grantee or contracting institution's existing Institutional Review Board or, if cooperation is on a frequent or continuing basis as between a medical school and a group of affiliated hospitals, appointments for extended periods may be made. All such cooperative arrangements must be approved by DHEW as part of a general assurance, or as an amendment to a general assurance.

(b) *Institutions with special assurances.* While responsibility for initial and continuing review necessarily lies with the grantee or contracting institution, DHEW may also require approved assurances from those cooperating institutions having immediate responsibility for subjects.

If the cooperating institution has on file with DHEW an approved general assurance, the grantee or contractor shall request the cooperating institution to conduct its own independent review of those aspects of the project or activity which will involve human subjects for which it has responsibility. Such a request shall be in writing and should provide for direct notification of the grantee's or contractor's Institutional Review Board in the event that the cooperating institution's Board finds the conduct of the activity to be unsatisfactory. If the cooperating institution does not have an approved general assurance on file with DHEW, it must submit to DHEW a general or special assurance which is determined by DHEW to comply with the provisions of this part.

The foregoing provision allows for a variety of procedures to be followed, when several institutions are engaged in activities under a grant or contract, to meet the review responsibilities under the regulations. Several specific requirements should be noted:

(1) the "grantee or prime contractor remains responsible for safeguarding the rights and welfare of subjects," even where the

subjects are involved in the activities under the aegis of cooperating institutions;

(2) all cooperative arrangements for interinstitutional joint review by institutions with general assurances must be approved as part of a general assurance or as an amendment to a general assurance; and

(3) each cooperating institution must have an approved general or special assurance.

INSTITUTIONAL EXECUTIVE RESPONSIBILITY

45 C.F.R. §46.118 Institution's executive responsibility
    Specific executive functions to be conducted by the institution include policy development and promulgation and continuing indoctrination of personnel. Appropriate administrative assistance and support shall be provided for the Board's functions. Implementation of the Board's recommendations through appropriate administrative action and followup is a condition of DHEW approval of an assurance. Board approvals, favorable actions, and recommendations are subject to review and to disapproval or further restriction by the institution officials. Board disapprovals, restrictions, or conditions cannot be rescinded or removed except by action of a Board described in the assurance approved by DHEW.

The effective performance of an Institutional Review Board requires the commitment of resources by the institutional administration. The cost of duplicating materials for distribution to the board including, for example, pertinent articles and copies of governmental regulations, is an institutional administrative cost. Other expenses attendant to the functioning of the board include the costs of secretarial and clerical services for the board chairman, attendance at seminars or meetings concerned with research issues by board members, preparation of materials for use at intrainstitutional meetings for the purpose of explaining and discussing the responsibilities of the board and the procedures it follows, and other informational services for institutional personnel concerned with research activities.

The significance of the responsibilities of the board is such that, unlike some faculty committees at academic institutions and some committees for various activities or purposes at other types of institutions, a clear support for board functions is essential to meet the requirements of the regulations. If problems with a study conducted at an institution were to materialize and allegations were made that poor board functioning (at least in part) was responsible, board members might well, in turn, assert that they were hampered or impeded because of the institutional administration's failure to provide assistance and support. Clearly, internal discord would exacerbate the difficulties and, where such assertions were founded in fact, precipitate sanctions by the Secretary of HEW. (See our later discussion of 45 C.F.R. §46.121.) By virtue of the submission of the institution's assurance, general or special, the obligations imposed by the regulations are assumed by the institution.

45 C.F.R. §46.119 Institution's records; confidentiality

(a) Copies of all documents presented or required for initial and continuing review by the Institutional Review Board, such as Board minutes, records of subject's consent, transmittals on actions, instruction, and conditions resulting from Board deliberations addressed to the activity director, are to be retained by the institution, subject to the terms and conditions of grant and contract awards.

(b) Except as otherwise provided by law information in the records or possession of an institution acquired in connection with an activity covered by this part, which information refers to or can be identified with a particular subject, may not be disclosed except:

(1) with the consent of the subject or his legally authorized representative; or

(2) as may be necessary for the Secretary to carry out his responsibilities under this part.

45 C.F.R. §46.120 Reports

Each institution with an approved assurance shall provide the Secretary with such reports and other information as the Secretary may from time to time prescribe.

The institution must establish procedures for retention of records of board activities and communications to it and for maintaining the confidentiality of information concerning particular subjects. Institutional policy can be stricter than is required by the regulations or the terms of a particular grant or contract. In addition to any requirements for retention of material in a contract or grant, the risk of liability litigation alone calls for policies and practices for retention of both board-related material and information concerning subjects that takes into consideration the statute of limitations of the state for personal injury actions, with particular thought given to (1) extensions of the period in which suit may be brought where minors or mental incompetents were subjects; (2) state legislation and regulations of state agencies regarding retention of records of patient care, when studies are conducted on patients in institutions; and (3) other retention requirements imposed by federal or state laws or regulations.

Confidentiality requirements imposed by federal or state legislation or regulations can also be stricter than those set forth in section 46.119(b). For example, regulations concerning records of patients treated for drug and alcohol abuse prohibit disclosure of information, except in limited circumstances, and require that patient consent to disclosure be in writing. [See 42 C.F.R. §§2.1 to 2.67-1; 40 *Federal Register* 27802 *et seq.* (July 1, 1975).]

EFFECT OF INSTITUTIONAL FAILURES TO COMPLY

45 C.F.R. §46.121 Early termination of awards; evaluation of subsequent applications and proposals

(a) If, in the judgment of the Secretary an institution has failed materially to comply with the terms of this policy with respect to a particular DHEW grant or contract, he may require that said grant or contract be terminated or suspended in the manner prescribed in applicable grant or procurement regulations.

(b) In evaluating applications or proposals for support of activities covered by this part, the Secretary may take into account, in addition to all other eligibility requirements and program criteria, such factors as: (1) whether the applicant or offeror has been subject to a termination or suspension under paragraph (a) of this section, (2) whether the applicant or offeror or the person who would direct the scientific and technical aspects of an activity has in the judgment of the Secretary failed materially to discharge his, her, or its responsibility for the protection of the rights and welfare of subjects in his, her, or its care (whether or not DHEW funds were involved), and (3) whether, where past deficiencies have existed in discharging such responsibility, adequate steps have in the judgment of the Secretary been taken to eliminate these deficiencies.

The sanctions that can be imposed by the Secretary of HEW include termination or suspension of an existing grant or contract when there has been material failure to comply with the policy regarding protection of human subjects. Evaluation of applications or proposals can include, in addition to other requirements and criteria, past performance of the institution and its personnel in meeting requirements for protection of human subjects.

It is particularly noteworthy that performance in regard to human subject protection in activities not funded by the DHEW can also be considered in the evaluation of subsequent applications and proposals. Thus, the issue of whether to review and process all protocols through procedures which, at minimum, are in conformity with the regulations regardless of source of funding, is clearly raised. If a less stringent set of requirements is used for activities not supported by the DHEW and failure to protect subjects' welfare and rights occurs, the effect could be to jeopardize the opportunity to secure future DHEW support. The position suggested in Chapter 2 and 3 is that the institution adopt a single set of review procedures and requirements and not distinguish among studies on the basis of source of funds, recognizing that some specific types of studies, such as deception studies, could necessitate modified procedures and consent requirements.

INSTITUTIONAL SANCTIONS FOR FAILURE TO PROTECT THE INTERESTS AND WELFARE OF SUBJECTS

As would be expected, federal regulations are silent on the matter of disciplining investigators and their staff personnel who violate policies and undertakings regarding research with human subjects. The institutional administration has an enforcement function in that, as a result of activities of the Institutional Review Board, complaints from subjects, or information obtained by the administrator assigned to maintain contact with the board, disciplinary action might have to be taken. Universities, hospitals, and governmental agencies, as well as other institutions, have procedures that must be followed in the disposition of allegations of improper performance of staff.

Violations of institutional policy, unauthorized disclosures of information, failures to report increased risks to subjects, or other improper conduct can lead to serious implications for the institution in addition to adverse effects on subjects. Furthermore, in keeping with the spirit if not the letter of the federal regulations, reporting the results of investigations and disciplinary action to the DHEW is advisable when the conduct of research supported by the DHEW has given rise to such action. Federal regulations are specific; the institution assumes the responsibility for protection of the welfare of subjects. The institution, therefore, must not only adopt policies and oversee procedures to protect subjects but must also enforce its policies to meet its responsibilities fully.

RISK MANAGEMENT AND INSURANCE PROTECTION

Considerable risks arise from research involving human subjects. The responsibility devolves on the institutional administration to determine which risks should be insured against, where insurance protection is to be secured, the appropriate limits of coverage for the insureds under each insurance policy, and the allocation of insurance costs within the institution. The DHEW regulations concerning protection of human subjects do not require (or for that matter even mention) insurance protection or compensation to subjects who suffer harm as a result of participation in research. The only section of the regulations that contains specific recognition of liability for harm being suffered by subjects provides as follows:

> **45 C.F.R. §46.109 Obligation to obtain informed consent; prohibition of exculpatory clauses**
> Any institution proposing to place any subject at risk is obligated to obtain and document legally effective informed consent. No such informed consent, oral or written, obtained under an assurance provided pursuant to this part shall include any exculpatory language through which the subject is made to waive, or to appear to waive, any of his legal rights, including any release of the institution or its agents from liability for negligence.

Thus, exculpatory language is barred from "informed oral or written" consent, required by the regulations. Apart from this prohibition, any exculpatory clause waiving legal rights to recover for harm suffered as a result of negligence prior to participation in a study would be of doubtful enforceability in a court of law in practically all, if not all, states today. The prohibition on exculpatory language would not necessarily apply to a contractual agreement between the institution and a subject to submit all claims for harm to arbitration.   Neither would it necessarily apply to an agreement between the subject and the institution under which the latter was obligated to provide stated compensation for harm suffered, regardless of whether negligence or malpractice occurred, in the conduct of the research, and that the former accept such compensation in lieu of seeking recovery of damages in court.   However, the legal status of arbitration and stated compensation agreements depends on state law, which must be reviewed by the institution's counsel if consideration is given to offering those options to subjects.

Liability Insurance

Not every injury to or poor outcome of a subject in a study can be attributed to participation in the study.   Furthermore not every injury or poor outcome from participation in a study would lead to imposition of liability if the subject were to institute suit under existing tort law concepts.   Liability for negligence or malpractice could be imposed only where the subject could show that the harm resulted from a deviation from the standard of care which, for studies regarding clinical practice, would be the prevailing standard for medical or professional performance.   The elements of damage recognized in such litigation would include medical and hospital expenses already incurred and those anticipated in the future, loss of income, and pain and suffering.   Under some circumstances a subject's spouse would have a right of action for loss of consortium; and, where the subject's death was caused by negligence or malpractice, his dependents ordinarily would be able to recover for their loss of support that otherwise would have been provided by the deceased.

This risk of liability for the investigator, the members of his staff, and the institution is essentially the same as that which the physician, other personnel involved in patient care, and health care institutions ordinarily encounter in providing purely therapeutic services.   However, there is an additional concern in the research context in that, in many situations (such as where an experimental procedure in place of the usual therapy is utilized or where the usual therapy is withheld without any other therapy being given) there is a departure from prevailing standards for medical and professional performance.   The few court decisions mentioned in Chapter 1, which gave rise to the concept that one experiments at his peril and is liable for any harm that follows, suggest that liability would be imposed for any harm suffered, when the procedure or other therapy is different from the prevailing standards. However, those cases dealt with situations in which it appeared no consent from the subjects had been obtained. It well could be that liability would not be imposed where the risks that materialized had been disclosed to the subjects, and the subjects then had agreed to participate. Without speculating further on the extent of the risk of liability for negligence or malpractice here, it is evident that the risk of liability is one for which insurance should be procured.

In addition to the investigator, his assisting staff, and the institution, who are at risk for negligence and malpractice, the Institutional Review Board and/or its individual members could also be faced with the risk of liability. The extent to which liability could be imposed where it could be shown that the board failed to make a proper inquiry into or review of a proposed study, or failed to fulfill its continuing or periodic review responsibility and the conduct of the study caused harm to subjects, is not clear and probably is limited. However, one function of liability insurance coverage that is particularly pertinent here is that the insurer undertakes to defend any suit brought against persons insured under the policy for claims within the policy coverage. The financial cost of defense of a lawsuit is often great and beyond the means of most persons, even if ultimate success in court is almost certain. Just as many hospitals and other health care institutions today secure insurance protection for members of their medical audit and other committees from risks of liability stemming from the performance of committee duties, so should insurance protection be secured for the members of the Institutional Review Board and for the institutional administrators who, on behalf of the institution, have the responsibility for continuing oversight of board performance.

Complex questions regarding insurance coverage are often present when investigators from one institution conduct a study involving subjects who are clients or patients of a separate institution. Under many circumstances where harm is asserted to have resulted from participation in a study, both institutions will be named as defendants in the ensuing litigation. It is essential that an institution seeking to secure protection from liability risks be certain that its insurance coverage encompasses all anticipated risks and, further, that investigators, who are not its employees but who are using its facilities or are involving its clients or patients as subjects, have adequate insurance coverage, either personally or through their employer institutions.

The discussion of liability risks above is directed primarily at situations in which at least some subjects are receiving therapeutic benefits. There are, however, additional situations that need to be mentioned. For example, in research to determine the effects of exertion or of heat or cold on body functions, there is always some risk present. If a subject who had given informed consent were to suffer harm as the result of the materialization of a described risk, under the present tort law system there would probably be no basis for liability, absent a showing that some or all the harm suffered resulted from failure by the investigator and others involved with the study to limit the risk to the extent reasonably possible under the circumstances. The key issue would be what steps were necessary to meet the standard of reasonableness in a particular context. Thus, failure to have first aid equipment available or a qualified person near enough to deal promptly with problems anticipated to arise would be the basis for liability if there were expert testimony attesting to the need for, and reasonableness of, such precautions to minimize the harm from risks of the research activity.

In addition to anticipated risks, there are some risks that cannot be described to prospective subjects in the consent process because they cannot be or are not anticipated. Even without a detailed legal analysis, harm from the materialization of such risks can be recognized as creating a serious risk of liability. It is possible that in litigation involving harm from an unanticipated risk, courts would be inclined to hold the investigator and the institution liable on a theory of strict liability and not require that negligence be shown, particularly where the subject was not warned prior to giving such consent, that there were risks that could not be predicted.

Benefits and Compensation for Subjects

Harm of some nature can be suffered by subjects as a result of participation in a study although there has been no fault or negligence on the part of the investigator, the study staff, or the institution. In the absence of fault or negligence, the injured subject ordinarily would not be able to succeed in litigation; however, the harm suffered by that subject can be just as real as that of the subject who is able to establish a basis for success in court.

The institutional administration has the option of providing compensation and benefits (hereinafter referred to as "benefits") to injured subjects without regard to whether they have meritorious legal claims. The adoption of such a policy, if benefits are sufficient to eliminate financial losses for subjects, could serve to reduce the likelihood that injured subjects would institute litigation for harm suffered as the result of participation in research, even where the prospect for successful litigation was good. A policy of this nature can be effectuated by securing insurance coverage which will provide benefits to the subjects depending on the harm or injury sustained by them. It is possible to self-insure to provide benefits in conformity with such a policy or to decline to adopt such a policy on behalf of subjects generally, which still leaves open the option to provide assistance to injured subjects on an ad hoc basis.

In the evaluation of the pros and cons concerning the issue of whether to provide benefits to subjects, one basic element of research activity must be kept clearly in mind; namely, research is conducted for the benefit of others—society and, as a practical matter, the investigator and his institution. Although in much clinical research the subject is a patient who could also derive benefits from participation in the study, there are potential benefits to others from his participation. In some research activity no benefits, actual or potential, can be assumed to exist for the subject. Therefore, if the risk of injury or poor outcome attributable to participation in a research activity is put on the subject and his family only, an element of unfairness is plainly discernable.

Although there have been proposals for a national system for providing benefits to subjects suffering harm from participation in research activities, the near future does not hold much promise for one to be instituted. Thus, it devolves on the institution to make its own decision, based on its notion of fairness with regard to where the financial burden of the harm should fall. The relative absence of litigation arising out of research activity could perhaps be indicative of the willingness of institutions to recognize and accept responsibilities for harm to subjects, but this is only conjecture.

Assuming that an institution decides to provide benefits to subjects without regard to liability, a great many questions must be resolved before putting such a policy into effect.

What benefits should be provided to injured subjects?
Among the elements of harm for which recovery of damages is recognized in litigation by an injured person are medical and hospital care, loss of income and future earning loss, and pain and suffering. In addition, a spouse can have an action for loss of consortium or loss of services. Where death has occurred, the dependents have economic interests that are recognized as the basis for recovery of damages.

The institution might adopt a policy with regard to benefits for subjects (and, where death has occurred, to their dependents) of a limited nature, of a liberal nature, or somewhere between these extremes. The approach of most workmen's compensation legislation offers a point of departure for decisions as to the extent and nature of benefits an institution should provide. Under workmen's compensation, medical, hospital, and rehabilitation care are ordinarily provided with few limits. Benefits for loss of income are set on a scale related to the injured's prior earnings up to a stated maximum, and fixed sums are payable for partial and total disability and for death. Pain and suffering and loss of consortium are among elements of harm that are not recognized for payment under workmen's compensation. The limits on amounts of benefits and compensation in workmen's compensation programs in many states might well be below the limits an institution, willing to establish this type of program, concludes to be fair treatment of injured subjects.

(2) *Will insurance be the vehicle for providing some or all the benefits?* The answer to this question depends on the availability of insurance for the elements of harm that can be anticipated from studies conducted by or at the institution. A hospital or other health services provider might be inclined not to secure insurance to cover medical and hospital care for injured subjects, seeing itself able to absorb that cost within its operating expenses. With a strong trend toward more precise cost allocation techniques in health services institutions, partly at the insistence of third-party payors, it might be advisable to secure such insurance. Also, should the subject be cared for elsewhere, either because he no longer will accept services at the institution where he was harmed or because the services he requires are not available at that institution, the costs of services to the subject will have to be paid directly. Funded self-insurance could be considered a mechanism for covering medical and hospital care.

The other elements of harm (most important, loss of income resulting from disability, and death benefits) call for an insurance approach, either with the purchase of insurance coverage or through funded self-insurance.

(3) *Should payments made and benefits provided, under a benefits program without regard to fault, be linked to individual and institutional liability insurance?* Under the "collateral source" rule, which is followed in most states, there is no reduction in the amount of damages that a person or institution held liable and/or its insurer must pay to the injured person for benefits provided or compensation paid pursuant to health and medical insurance for the benefit of the injured person. This leads to a potential double payment for some elements of harm. Most health and medical insurance companies in their policies provide for a right of subrogation, which will allow them to institute suit to recover their costs when the injured patient has a

right of action against another person, and to recover their costs where the injured party receives payment or becomes entitled to payment from the person who caused the harm by the settlement of a claim or recovery of damages by litigation.

It is clearly to the advantage of an institution with a benefits program, to the extent legally possible, to avoid double payment to the injured subject and thereby eliminate the costs of such payment. One method that might be employed to accomplish this result would be to restrict the eligibility to receipt of program benefits to subjects who agree in advance to subrogation. This would be a condition before a subject became an insured or a beneficiary under the insurance policy. Another technique would be to require that a subject agree to accept the benefits program as an exclusive remedy before becoming eligible to receive those benefits, at least for such elements of harm as were included in that program. If the agreement were to purport to eliminate all legal rights of action, the document embodying the agreement might raise the issue of the exculpatory clause, barred by the DHEW regulations. The effect of refusal by the subject to agree in both instances would be that he would retain his legal rights to seek and obtain remedies in court as he might otherwise possess, but he would not be entitled to program benefits for harm suffered regardless of the presence of fault or negligence. Possible mechanisms to avoid or limit double payment must be considered in light of applicable law and options available through insurers.

(4) *Should arbitration or some other method of determination be provided for in the benefits program to resolve issues of whether, and to what extent, harm suffered resulted from participation in the research activity rather than other causes, such as the normal progress of the disease from which the subject-patient was suffering?* The causation issue is one present in both the liability and the benefits program contexts. Medical opinion is mixed on this question. Since one objective of the benefits program is to eliminate or reduce resort to the courts, employing another method for resolving causation issues might be advisable. A requirement for nonjudicial resolution of causation issues could only be brought into operation with the agreement of the subject.

(5) *Should a separate benefits program be established for each research activity, or should a single one be applicable to all research activities?* Investigation to find an answer to this question must encompass considerations of cost. Although a single program provided by insurance could simplify administration, the premium cost of securing insurance on a yearly basis might be greater than would be for individual coverage for each research activity. With yearly

coverage for all research activity, the premium must be set to cover research that as yet is unapproved and the financial risks of which cannot be estimated. This would promote higher premium costs. But one consideration in favor of a single benefits program covering all research activity during a specified time period, particularly when insurance is to be sought, is the danger that no insurance coverage will be obtainable for a specific study, as the insurer seeks to avoid risks of financial responsibility that are difficult to estimate.

(6) *How should the costs of providing the benefits program be borne or allocated?* A number of considerations enter into this decision. First, where funded research is involved, it may be possible to have the granting agency or sponsor include the cost of insurance premiums as a direct expense of the research. This would, in essence, be a pass-through of the cost; and it can be argued that the premium cost is no different from any other expense necessary for the proper conduct of the research, given the concern about the rights and interests of the subjects. From the point of view of the institution this ordinarily would appear to be the preferred method, but granting agencies and sponsors often are not willing to accept insurance premium costs as a direct research expense. Second, the insurance premium costs could be included in calculating the institution's overhead rate, which is recognized by funding sources. However, some foundations and other entities that fund research refuse to pay overhead on their grants. This would mean that, at least in regard to research activities such funding sources sponsor, the insurance premium cost attributable to those research activities would not be received even indirectly from the sponsors. Third, some research activity is conducted without direct financial support, particularly student projects to fulfill degree and other academic requirements. Where there is one benefits program covering all research activity conducted at the institution, no particular problem is raised. However, where there is no single program, the institution would have to find a source of funds to pay the insurance premium costs associated with such unfunded research activities. These costs could be included in the expenses used to calculate the general overhead rate and thereby be recoverable through overhead payments. They also could be treated as instructional costs, and the responsible departments of the institution would be required to include them in their operating budgets.

A final consideration concerns which method is likely to promote the most effective institutional administrative review of research activities, including the performance of the Institutional Review Board in taking action and imposing requirements protecting interests of

subjects. When the insurance premium cost is included as a direct
expense on a grant or contract, it may be argued that the incentive
for institutional administrative review is less than where it is an
indirect cost recaptured, to some extent, through the overhead rate.
The latter might tend to bring about closer surveillance by the
institution of research activities as a whole, particularly where a
single benefits program existed, because changes in premium cost on
an institutional basis would have a more visible impact on the budget
of the entire institution.

5

THE SCOPE OF LAW RELATING TO INVESTIGATIONS WITH HUMAN SUBJECTS

The various aspects of the institutional review process and federal regulations requiring its use have been our emphasis so far. Though some mention of other legal requirements has been made, it is this chapter that is devoted to a survey of law, which has had or could have an impact on the conduct of research with human subjects. The range of relevant and potentially relevant legal material is discussed here by way of example, rather than as a set of references. Some material is pertinent only to a specific potential subject population or a specific type of research activity. Several of the legal concepts mentioned here ordinarily would be of practical concern only if elements of the protocol were not followed or if conduct generally regarded as wrongful occurred in the course of a research study.

One must keep in mind that new legislation, regulations, court decisions, opinions of attorneys-general, and other legal materials will continue to appear; and that they will affect the conduct of individual investigators and institutions. The responsibility for bringing new requirements to the attention of the institutional administration so the board and investigators can be made aware of them is that of the institution's legal counsel.

FEDERAL LAWS AND REGULATIONS

The federal government regulates specific types of research either through its control over the distribution of drugs or through its control over funding. The DHEW regulations so frequently cited in Chapters 2, 3, and 4 are but one element of the federal regulation of research involving human subjects.

Food and Drug Administration

The FDA extensively regulates research involving drugs (21 C.F.R. §312.1) pursuant to the 1962 Food and Drug Amendments (52 Stat. 1051-1055). It indirectly influences the design of research by virtually requiring controlled studies as part of the proof of efficacy before approving new drug applications (21 C.F.R. §314.111(a)(5). Several of the most important aspects of the law dealing with research involving drugs are discussed as an example.

Sponsor.—A sponsor (the manufacturer) needs studies on humans conducted with a new drug as a necessary step toward approval for its promotion and sale. The FDA requires submission of a "Notice of Claimed Investigational Exemption for a New Drug" before research on humans can begin. [Form FD-1571, which appears at 21 C.F.R. §312.1(a)(2)]. If the FDA does not request that the drug continue to be withheld or restricted within thirty days of that notice, the drug can be delivered to investigators for use in investigational studies described in the notice. The notice must include, among other information, all data from preclinical investigations (animal studies) and any existing clinical studies or experience (usually from other countries), the names and qualifications (scientific training and experience) of investigators (with a statement that each has signed a Form FD-1572 or FD-1573), an outline of the phases of the planned investigations, and a description of the institutional review committee, which must review the clinical study if it is to be conducted "on institutionalized subjects" or "by an individual affiliated with an institution which agrees to assume responsibility for the study."

Ordinarily, there are three phases to the investigations. Phase 1 is the introduction of the drug into man to determine human toxicity, metabolism, absorption, elimination, other pharmacological action, preferred route of administration, and safe dosage range. Normal subjects are used for this phase. Phase 2 is the introduction into a limited number of patients for specific disease control or prophylaxis. Phases 1 and 2 sometimes overlap; sometimes additional animal studies are required before phase 3 can begin. Phase 3 is the clinical trial in groups of subjects with a given disease or condition to assess the drug's safety, effectiveness, and optimum dose schedule for diagnosis, treatment, or prophylaxis. This phase must be designed to produce well-controlled data.

The institutional review committee must be composed of members with "varying backgrounds, ... lawyers, clergymen, or laymen as well as scientists." Neither the sponsor nor the investigator can participate in the membership selection. The committee cannot "allow participation in its review and conclusions by any individual involved in the conduct of the research activity under review (except to provide information to the committee)." The investigator must report "any emergent problems, serious adverse reactions, or proposed procedural changes" to the committee. The committee must review each study at least annually, and documentation is required. The signing of Form FD-1571 entails an assurance of all the above.

If the institution has an accepted "general assurance" in accordance with 45 C.F.R. Part 46 on file with the DHEW, review by that institutional review board according to its procedures is accepted in lieu of the FDA assurance and procedure. A statement that an accepted "general assurance" is on file should be provided with FD-1571, if this option is applicable and desired.

The sponsor has a continuing responsibility to monitor the study. The FDA, in addition, has the authority to investigate periodically institutions to determine whether the assurances are being met.

If the study is to be conducted in a foreign country, in lieu of FD-1571 a formal request to allow drug shipment must be made by the government of the country where the drug is to be received. The request must specify that the government has adequate information about the drug and the study and that the drug may be legally used by the consignee in that country. When clinical data generated outside the United States and not subject to a "Notice of Claimed Investigational Exemption for a New Drug" are to be submitted to the FDA to help establish the safety and effectiveness of the drug, the requirements of 21 C.F.R. §312.20 (40 *Federal Register* 16056, April 9, 1975) must be met, which, among others, requires compliance with the Declaration of Helsinki, an internationally recognized statement concerning protection of research subjects.

The sponsor must monitor the research, collect data, and at least annually submit progress reports to the FDA. There are requirements for notifying the FDA of significant hazards, contraindications, sideeffects, and precautions. The investigation must be discontinued promptly if a sufficiently serious finding should occur. If an investigator repeatedly or deliberately fails to maintain or make available his records, the sponsor must discontinue deliveries to that investigator.

Investigator.—Form FD-1572, which investigators involved in phase 1 or phase 2 studies must sign, must include the investigator's qualifications (education and training), the name and address of the research facility, an assurance of institutional review (under the same circumstances, in the same form, and with the same option of the 45 C.F.R. Part 46 institutional review board review as the sponsor has), the estimated duration of the project, the maximum number of subjects, a general outline of the project, and agreements that certain records will be kept (including case histories), that certain periodic and immediate reports will be made to the sponsor, that the drugs will be administered only under the personal supervision of the principal investigator or one of his investigators listed on the form as being responsible to him, that the drugs will not be supplied to others, and, if the study involves institutionalized subjects, that it will not be commenced until committee approval is obtained. In addition the investigator must certify that

> he will inform any patients or any persons used as controls, or their representatives, that drugs are being used for investigational purposes, and will obtain the consent of the subjects, or their representatives, except where this is not feasible or, in the investigator's professional judgment, is contrary to the best interests of the subjects. 21 C.F.R. §312.1

The consent requirement has been interpreted in a statement of policy that appears at 21 C.F.R. §310.102. It provides that consent must be obtained in *all* cases where the drug is "administered primarily for the accumulation of scientific knowledge" and in all cases where the drug is administered to "patients under treatment," unless the patient's situation falls within an *exceptional* case, "exceptional" being defined in a restrictive sense. "Not feasible" and "best interests" are also defined to limit the circumstances where they will lead to not obtaining consent. The requirements for consent include legal capacity, voluntariness ("so situated as to be able to exercise free power of choice"), and a "fair explanation of pertinent information," that is,

> the investigator should carefully consider and make known to him (taking into consideration such person's well-being and

his ability to understand) the nature, expected duration and purpose of the administration of said investigational drug; the method and means by which it is to be administered; the hazards involved; the existence of alternative forms of therapy, if any; and the beneficial effects upon his health or person that might possibly come from administration of the investigational drug. 21 C.F.R. §310.102(h).

Written consent must be obtained from subjects of phase 1 and phase 2 studies. In phase 3 studies, if necessary after taking into consideration the physical and mental state of the patient, oral consent can be substituted and recorded in the medical chart.

Form FD-1573, which investigators involved in phase 3 studies must sign, must include more detailed information concerning the investigator's qualifications, the clinical facilities involved, if any, and the plan of investigation. The same agreements as in FD-1572 must be made.

Of particular interest in the regulations pertaining to investigations of drugs is the provision setting forth the principles constituting "the essentials of adequate and well-controlled clinical investigations." [See 21 C.F.R. §314.111(a)(5)]. These state that the protocol for the study must include a clear statement of its objectives, a method of subject selection that minimizes bias and assures comparability in test and control groups of pertinent variables, an explanation of the methods of observation and recording of results, and a provision for a comparison of results that permits quantitative evaluation.

Repeated or deliberate failure to comply with the conditions of FD-1572 or FD-1573 or repeated or deliberate submission of false information to the sponsor can disqualify the investigator from receiving investigational drugs. An informal hearing is available before disqualification. All studies by such an investigator are under suspicion, and all data from that investigator are carefully examined. An investigator can be reinstated as eligible if the FDA commissioner is satisfied there will be compliance in the future. [See 21 C.F.R. §312.1(c)].

There is a procedure for terminating the exemption and, thus, ending all clinical studies with the drug, if one of eleven types of violations occurs. [See 21 C.F.R. §312.1(d)].

If the study involves biologics (products licensed under 42 U.S.C. §§201 *et seq.*), the Bureau of Biologics has responsibility for the regulation of that research. The same procedure and forms as the

FDA's are used, but with "Bureau of Biologics" substituted for "Food and Drug Administration."

National Research Act (P. L. 93-348)

National Commission for the Protection of Human Subjects of Biomedical and Behavioral Research (NCPHS).—Part A of Title II of the National Research Act, signed July 12, 1974, established the NCPHS, to be appointed by the Secretary of HEW. The commission was given an extensive charge, including to "identify the basic ethical principles which should underlie the conduct of biomedical and behavioral research involving human subjects, . . . develop guidelines which should be followed in such research to assure that it is conducted in accordance with such principles," and make "recommendations" for appropriate administrative action by the DHEW. The recommendations are to be published in the *Federal Register* for comment. The secretary must publish his reasons for adopting a policy different from the recommendation.

In carrying out its charge, the commission must consider the following:

(i) The boundaries between biomedical or behavioral research involving human subjects and the accepted and routine practice of medicine.

(ii) The role of assessment of risk-benefit criteria in the determination of the appropriateness of research involving human subjects.

(iii) Appropriate guidelines for the selection of human subjects for participation in biomedical and behavioral research.

(iv) The nature and definition of informed consent in various research settings.

(v) Mechanisms for evaluating and monitoring the performance of Institutional Review Boards ... and appropriate enforcement mechanisms for carrying out their decisions.

The commission was given several other tasks, including identifying the requirements for informed consent to participation for children, prisoners, and the institutionalized mentally infirm; defining the circumstances under which fetal research can be conducted; recommending policies defining the circumstances under which psychosurgery is appropriate; determining whether research not subject to regulation by the DHEW should be controlled to protect subjects and, if so, developing and recommending a mechanism; and studying the "ethical, social, and legal implications of advances in biomedical and behavioral research and technology."

The commission has a twenty-four-month life by law. As of March 1, 1976, the only regulations emanating from its work concern fetal research. The National Research Act imposed a ban on DHEW-funded research "on a living human fetus, before or after the induced abortion of such fetus, unless such research is done for the purpose of assuring survival of the fetus." This ban was to last until the NCPHS made recommendations to the DHEW concerning proper conduct of such research. The commission made its recommendations on May 21, 1975. The DHEW published its regulations covering fetuses, pregnant women, and human *in vitro* fertilization on August 8, 1975, incorporating some changes from the recommendations of the Commission. (See 45 C.F.R. §§46.201-211; 40 *Federal Register* 33526-530). The contents of the regulations are outlined in Chapter 3. It should be noted that the regulations do not preempt state laws, which can be more restrictive.

National Advisory Council for the Protection of Subjects of Biomedical and Behavioral Research.—Part B of Title II authorized the establishment of the advisory council as a continuing group to advise the secretary of HEW on matters "pertaining to the protection of human subjects of biomedical and behavioral research." Among its statutory functions are review of "policies, regulations and other requirements" of DHEW, particularly in regard to their effectiveness, and review of research to determine the need for changes in "policies, regulations and requirements" of the DHEW. The foregoing indicates that the DHEW regulations concerning research involving human subjects are in evolution.

STATE LAWS AND REGULATIONS

Several states have passed legislation and have promulgated regulations with substantial impact on some aspects of investigations with human subjects. However, except for one New York statute, these legal materials are not as encompassing as federal legal materials and tend to focus on specific matters rather than to establish procedures for institutional review of research activities.

Drugs

State law ordinarily requires that, prior to the use of any investigational new drug, an application for its use be filed with a state

agency indicating that there is a current "Notice of Claimed Investigational Exemption for a New Drug" filed with the FDA.
Certain specific additional information concerning the investigation
is often required. The following is an example of such a statutory
provision.

**Ill. Ann. Stat. Tit. 56½, §517 (Supp. 1975) New drugs
—Application for introduction into interstate commerce—Exceptions**

*   *   *

(b) No person shall use in human beings or animals a new
drug limited to investigational use unless the person has (1)
filed with the Federal Food and Drug Administration a
completed and signed application "Notice of claimed investigational exemption for a new drug" in accordance with
Section 130.3 and 130.3a of Title 21 of the Code of Federal
Regulations and the exemption has not been terminated and
(2) filed with the Director, if any portion of the human or
animal investigation is conducted in the State of Illinois, a
form including but not limited to the following information:
(a) name of person conducting the investigation; (b) type of
drugs or chemicals used; (c) subjects (human or animal) of
investigation; (d) location of investigation; and (e) purpose
and expected results of investigation; such form shall be
prescribed and furnished by the Department; and (3) the
drug shall be plainly labeled in compliance with Section
505(i) or 507(d) of the Federal Act.

For many state institutions specific legislation or departmental
regulations exist, which set forth the duties of departmental and
institutional administrators. In some states there are specific duties
concerning research in various institutions. The following Illinois
provision requires the authorization of the Director of Mental Health
and Developmental Disabilities before certain drugs can be used for
research purposes at public mental institutions in Illinois.

**Ill. Ann. Stat. Tit. 91½, §100-5.1 (Supp. 1975) Prescription of
drugs to be administered in institutions**

The Director shall prescribe by regulation lists of drugs
that may be administered in institutions under the jurisdiction of the Department. The Director may, in the regulations, establish maximum prescription dosages and conditions necessary for the administration of any drug or type of

drug and may establish maximum time limits for the prescription of any drug or type of drug after which time the prescription shall terminate unless reissued. Regulations issued under this paragraph shall be reviewed annually, and may remain effective only for 15 months unless reissued.

Drugs not listed by the Director may not be administered in institutions under the jurisdiction of the Department, provided that an unlisted drug may be administered as part of research with the prior written consent of the Director specifying the nature of the permitted use and the physicians authorized to prescribe the drug. Drugs, as used in this Section, mean psychotropic and narcotic drugs.

State controlled substances laws, which are concerned mainly with drug abuse, frequently refer to research in connection with the maintenance of confidentiality of information concerning the use of controlled substances by individuals. The following excerpts of Iowa statutory provisions illustrate such legislation.

Iowa Code Ann. §§204.504 (Supp. 1975) Co-operative arrangements and confidentiality

1. The department and board, subject to approval and direction of the governor, shall co-operate with federal and other state agencies in discharging its responsibilities concerning traffic in controlled substances and in suppressing the abuse of controlled substances. To this end, they may jointly:

*   *   *

c. Co-operate with the bureau by establishing a centralized unit which will accept, catalogue, file, and collect statistics, including records of drug dependent persons and other controlled substance law offenders within the state, and make such information available for federal, state and local law enforcement purposes; except that they shall not furnish the name or identity of a patient or research subject whose indentity could not be obtained under subsection 3.

*   *   *

3. A practitioner engaged in medical practice or research or the Iowa drug abuse authority or any program which is licensed by the authority shall not be required to furnish the name or identity of a patient or research subject to the board or the department, nor shall the practitioner or the authority or any program which is licensed by the authority be com-

pelled in any state or local civil, criminal, administrative, legislative or other proceedings to furnish the name or identity of an individual that the practitioner or the authority or any of its licensed programs is obligated to keep confidential.

§ 204.505   Forfeitures
1. The following are subject to forfeiture:

*   *   *

d. All books, records, and research products and materials, including formulas, microfilm, tapes, and data which are used, or intended for use, in violation of this chapter.
2. Property subject to forfeiture under this chapter may be seized by the board or department when:
a. The seizure is incident to an arrest or a search under a search warrant or an inspection under an administrative inspection warrant;
b. The property subject to seizure has been the subject of a prior judgment in favor of the state in a criminal injunction or forfeiture proceeding based upon this chapter;
c. The department has probable cause to believe that the property is directly or indirectly dangerous to health or safety; or
d. The department has probable cause to believe that the property was used or is intended to be used in violation of this chapter.

Specific legislation in some states exist to facilitate and monitor the research use of certain drugs. In the California provisions below, which are part of the state's controlled substances legislation, the composition, procedures, and responsibilities of a group to advise on research with marijuana and hallucinogenic drugs is stated.

Cal. Health and Safety Code (1975)

§ 11480   Marijuana and hallucinogenic drug research;
research advisory panel; hearings; projects
The Legislature finds that there is a need to encourage further research into the nature and effects of marijuana and hallucinogenic drugs and to coordinate research efforts on such subjects.
There is a Research Advisory Panel which consists of a representative of the State Department of Health, a repre-

sentative of the California State Board of Pharmacy, a representative of the Attorney General, a representative of the University of California who shall be a pharmacologist or physician or a person holding a doctorate degree in the health sciences, a representative of a private university in this state who shall be a pharmacologist or physician or a person holding a doctorate degree in the health sciences, a representative of a statewide professional medical society in this state who shall be engaged in the private practice of medicine and shall be experienced in treating controlled substance dependency, and a representative appointed by and serving at the pleasure of the Governor, who shall hold a doctorate degree in the health sciences and shall have experience in drug abuse or controlled substance research. The Governor shall annually designate the private university and the professional medical society represented on the panel. Members of the panel shall be appointed by the heads of the entities to be represented, and they shall serve at the pleasure of the appointing power.

The panel shall annually select a chairman from among its members.

The panel may hold hearings on, and in other ways study, research projects concerning marijuana or hallucinogenic drugs in this state. Members of the panel shall serve without compensation, but shall be reimbursed for any actual and necessary expenses incurred in connection with the performance of their duties.

The panel may approve research projects, which have been registered by the Attorney General, into the nature and effects of marijuana or hallucinogenic drugs, and shall inform the Attorney General of the head of such approved research projects which are entitled to receive quantities of marijuana pursuant to Section 11478.

The panel may withdraw approval of a research project at any time, and when approval is withdrawn shall notify the head of the research project to return any quantities of marijuana to the Attorney General.

The panel shall report annually to the Legislature and the Governor those research projects approved by the panel, the nature of each research project, and, where available, the conclusions of the research project.

§ 11481   Research adivsory panel; hearings and studies; project approval; reports

The Research Advisory Panel may hold hearings on, and in other ways study, research projects concerning the treatment of abuse of controlled substances.

The panel may approve research projects, which have been registered by the Attorney General, concerning the treatment of abuse of controlled substances and shall inform the chief of such approval. The panel may withdraw approval of a research project at any time and when approval is withdrawn shall so notify the chief.

The panel shall, annually and in the manner determined by the panel, report to the Legislature and the Governor those research projects approved by the panel, the nature of each research project, and where available, the conclusions of the research project.

§ 11603   Protection of persons who are subjects of research

The Attorney General, with the approval of the Research Advisory Panel, may authorize persons engaged in research on the use and effects of controlled substances to withhold the names and other identifying characteristics of individuals who are the subjects of the research. Persons who obtain this authorization are not compelled in any civil, criminal, administrative, legislative, or other proceeding to identify the individuals who are the subjects of research for which the authorization was obtained.

§ 11604   Authorized possession and use of controlled substances for research; immunity

The Attorney General, with the approval of the Research Advisory Panel, may authorize the possession and distribution of controlled substances by persons engaged in research. Persons who obtain this authorization are exempt from state prosecution for possession and distribution of controlled substances to the extent of the authorization.

Consent for Experiments with Humans

The research for this book has uncovered only one state, Louisiana, with a statutory provision that, by its terms, defines a crime of human experimentation.

La. Stat. Ann. Tit. 14, §87.2 (1974) Human experimentation

Human experimentation is the use of any live born human being, without consent of that live born human being, as hereinafter defined, for any scientific or laboratory research or any other kind of experimentation or study except to protect or preserve the life and health of said live born human being, or the conduct, on a human embryo or fetus in utero, of any experimentation or study except to preserve the life or to improve the health of said human embryo or fetus.

A human being is live born, or there is a live birth, whenever there is the complete expulsion or extraction from its mother of a human embryo or fetus, irrespective of the duration of pregnancy, which after such separation, breathes or shows any other evidence of life such as beating of the heart, pulsation of the umbilical cord, or movement of voluntary muscles, whether or not the umbilical cord has been cut or the placenta is attached.

Whoever commits the crime of human experimentation shall be imprisoned at hard labor for not less than five nor more than twenty years, or fined not more than ten thousand dollars, or both.

This provision illustrates how a statutory provision can create difficulties. It is evidently directed at a specific activity but is worded to apply to a much wider range of activities than its proponents might have envisioned. Human experimentation, as defined, is a crime punishable by substantial penalties. The use of any embryo, fetus, or live born human being without his consent for "any scientific or laboratory research or any other kind of experimentation or study" constitutes the crime, except for specified, limited experimental purposes.

The apparent objective of this provision is to restrict the use of any live product of an abortion in a research study. However, it extends a threat of criminal sanctions to any person who engages in any experimental activity not covered by the exception, no matter how slight the risk, when the subject is unable to give consent or refuses to consent. The words "live born human being" encompass all children and adults. Although the statute creates no particular problem for the conduct of research with competent adult subjects, it apparently proscribes research involving young children or adults incapable, mentally or physically, of giving consent. The statute does not recognize the possibility of a legal representative giving consent on behalf of such a subject, even where risks of harm are minimal or even nonexistent.

More than half the states have enacted legislation to facilitate the treatment of minors by declaring the consent of certain minors to be sufficient for authorizing necessary medical and other health services. Age, marital status, and the presence of specified conditions are factors in such legislation, which allow the minor's consent to be effective. Some research involves therapeutic measures that fall within the scope of those limited health services for which minor consent ordinarily is sufficient. However, the application of minor consent legislation in this context is not clear. A strong argument can be made for experimental participation under some circumstances: (1) where treatment is necessary, (2) where the procedure will be of benefit to the minor, and (3) where no alternative therapy of proven efficacy is available. The minor's ability to consent to medical and health services under this type of existing legislation could extend to authorizing an experimental procedure or participation in a study involving the innovative (not generally accepted) use of an established therapeutic measure. But the minor consent legislation does not deal specifically with this aspect, and it is doubtful that the states, in enacting such legislation, intended not to alter the traditional requirement of parental consent to participation in research.

Several provisions of the Pennsylvania minor consent legislation provide an example.

Pa. Stat. Ann. (Supp. 1975)
§ 10101 Individual Consent

Any minor who is eighteen years of age or older, or has graduated from high school, or has married, or has been pregnant, may give effective consent to medical, dental and health services for himself or herself, and the consent of no other person shall be necessary.

§ 10102   Consent for Children with Minor Parents
Any minor who has been married or has borne a child may give effective consent to medical, dental and health services for his or her child.

§ 10103   Pregnancy, Venereal Disease and Other Reportable Diseases
Any minor may give effective consent for medical and health services to determine the presence of or to treat

pregnancy, and venereal disease and other diseases reportable under the act of April 23, 1956 (P. L. 1510), known as the "Disease Prevention and Control Law of 1955," and the consent of no other person shall be necessary.

Fetal Research

Several states have enacted legislation limiting or forbidding research on live human fetuses and regulating research on dead fetuses. The Massachusetts provision is the most detailed example of such legislation. Prohibitions or restriction on fetal research are usually found in the state's abortion legislation, particularly abortion legislation enacted subsequent to the United States Supreme Court decisions limiting the conditions a state can impose on the performance of an abortion.

Mass. Gen. Laws Ann. Ch. 112, §12J (Supp. 1975) Experimentation on human fetuses prohibited; penalties

No person shall use any live human fetus, whether before or after expulsion from its mother's womb, for scientific, laboratory, research or other kind of experimentation. This section shall not prohibit procedures incident to the study of a human fetus while it is in its mother's womb, provided that in the best medical judgment of the physician, made at the time of the study, said procedures do not substantially jeopardize the life or health of the fetus, and provided said fetus is not the subject of a planned abortion. In any criminal proceeding the fetus shall be conclusively presumed not to be the subject of a planned abortion if the mother signed a written statement at the time of the study, that she was not planning an abortion.

This section shall not prohibit or regulate diagnostic or remedial procedures the purpose of which is to determine the life or health of the fetus involved or to preserve the life or health of the fetus involved or the mother involved.

A fetus is a live fetus for purposes of this section when, in the best medical judgment of a physician, it shows evidence of life as determined by the same medical standards as are used in determining evidence of life in a spontaneously aborted fetus at approximately the same stage of gestational development.

No experimentation may knowingly be performed upon a dead fetus unless the consent of the mother has first been obtained, provided however that such consent shall not be required in the case of a routine pathological study. In any criminal proceeding, consent shall be conclusively presumed to have been granted for the purposes of this section by a written statement, signed by the mother who is at least eighteen years of age, to the effect that she consents to the use of her fetus for scientific, laboratory, research or other kind of experimentation or study; such written consent shall constitute lawful authorization for the transfer of the dead fetus.

No person shall perform or offer to perform an abortion where part or all of the consideration for said performance is that the fetal remains may be used for experimentation or other kind of research or study.

No person shall knowingly sell, transfer, distribute or give away any fetus for a use which is in violation of the provisions of this section. For purposes of this section, the word "fetus" shall include also an embryo or neonate.

Whoever violates the provisions of this section shall be punished by imprisonment in a jail or house of correction for not less than one year nor more than two and one half years or by imprisonment in the state prison for not more than five years.

The following excerpt from the Pennsylvania abortion legislation is more typical of the fetal research laws found in other states.

Pa. Stat. Ann. Tit. 35, §6605 (Supp. 1975) Protection of life of fetus

*   *   *

(b) No person shall use any premature infant aborted alive for any type of scientific, research, laboratory, or other kind of experimentation except as necessary to protect or preserve the life and health of such premature infant aborted alive.

(c) The department shall make regulations to provide for the humane disposition of dead fetuses.

(d) Any person who fails to make the determination provided for in subsection (a) of this section, or who fails to exercise the degree of professional skill, care and diligence or to provide the technique as provided for in subsection (a) of this section, or who violates subsection (b) of this section, shall be subject to such civil or criminal liability as would pertain to him had the fetus been a child who was intended to be born and not aborted.

Because statutory provisions concerning fetal research establish crimes that carry the possibility of substantial prison sentences, their scope and possible applicability to proposed research must be scrutinized carefully.

Research Coordination Function

The legislative mandate of a state agency, council, or department can include the specific function of coordinating research. Where such an entity has been granted this authority, regulations often exist to spell out how the coordination is to be effected. As a practical matter, limitations on research are imposed by such legislation or regulations. The following excerpts from the Pennsylvania statutory provisions concerning the Governor's Council on Drug and Alcohol Abuse illustrate such legislation; the specific concern with confidentiality evident in other legislation cited in this chapter is also found here and should be noted.

Pa. Stat. Ann. Tit. 71, 1690.104 (Supp. 1975) Council's powers and responsibilities

(a) The council shall develop and adopt a State plan for the control, prevention, treatment, rehabilitation, research, education, and training aspects of drug and alcohol abuse and dependence problems. The State plan shall include, but not be limited to, provision for:

(1) Coordination of the efforts of all State agencies in the control, prevention, treatment, rehabilitation, research, education, and training aspects of drug and alcohol abuse and dependence problems. It shall allocate functional responsibility for these aspects of the drug and alcohol abuse and dependence problems among the various State agencies so as to avoid duplications and inconsistencies in the efforts of the agencies.

(2) Coordination of all health and rehabilitation efforts to deal with the problem of drug and alcohol abuse and dependence, including, but not limited to, those relating to vocational rehabilitation, manpower development and training, senior citizens, law enforcement assistance, parole and probation systems, jails and prisons, health research facilities,

mental retardation facilities and community mental health centers, juvenile delinquency, health professions, educational assistance, hospital and medical facilities, social security, community health services, education professions development, higher education, Commonwealth employees health benefits, economic opportunity, comprehensive health planning, elementary and secondary education, highway safety and the civil service laws.

*   *   *

(7) Coordination of research, scientific investigations, experiments, and studies relating to the cause, epidemiology, sociological aspects, toxicology, pharmacology, chemistry, effects on health, dangers to public health, prevention, diagnosis and treatment of drug and alcohol abuse and dependence.

(8) Investigation of methods for the more precise detection and determination of alcohol and controlled substances in urine and blood samples, and by other means, and publication on a current basis of uniform methodology for such detections and determinations.

Any information obtained through scientific investigation or research conducted pursuant to this act shall be used in ways so that no name or identifying characteristics of any person shall be divulged without the approval of the council and the consent of the person concerned. Persons engaged in research pursuant to this section shall protect the privacy of individuals who are the subject of such research by withholding from all persons not connected with the conduct of such research the names or other identifying characteristics of such individuals. Persons engaged in such research shall protect the privacy of such individuals and may not be compelled in any Federal, State, civil, criminal, administrative, legislative, or other proceeding to identify such individuals.

*   *   *

(15) Grants and contracts from the appropriate State department or agency for the prevention and treatment of drug and alcohol dependence. The grants and contracts may include assistance to local governments and public and private agencies, institutions, and organizations for prevention, treatment, rehabilitation, research, education and training aspects of the drug and alcohol abuse and dependence prob-

lems with the Commonwealth. Any grant made or contract entered into by a department or agency shall be pursuant to the functions allocated to that department or agency by the State plan.

Inmates of Public Institutions

Issues concerning prisoners and other special population groups are discussed in Chapter 3. Some states have imposed, by statute, specific requirements or procedures to protect the interests of such persons.

The following provision from Iowa deals only with prisoner consent to serving as subjects.

Iowa Code Ann. §246.47 (1969) Patients for medical research
The state director may send to the hospital of the medical college of the state university inmates of the Iowa state penitentiary and the men's reformatory for medical research at the hospital. Before any inmate is sent to the medical college, he must volunteer his services in writing. An inmate may withdraw his consent at any time.

The prior history of the involvement of special populations in research with scant control or regulation has lead some states to establish an entity with the responsibility to review and supervise such operations. The jurisdiction and authority of the Medical Research Commission in the following Oklahoma legislation should be noted, particularly in regard to the handling and disposition of funds.

Okla. Stat. Ann. Tit. 63 (1973)

§ 47.1 Medical Research Commission—Creation—Membership
There is hereby created the Medical Research Commission to be composed of the Vice President for Medical Affairs at the University of Oklahoma, or his designate, who shall receive his appointment in writing, as Chairman; the Executive Vice President-Director of Research of the Oklahoma Medical Research Foundation; the Vice President-Director of Administration of the Oklahoma Medical Research Foundation; the Director of Mental Health, and the Commissioner of Public Health, as members to serve without pay other than necessary and actual expenses.

§ 47.2   Supervision of projects at state institutions

The Medical Research Commission shall have jurisdiction of the supervision and control of all medical research projects and programs which may be instigated or proposed for the testing or experiment of any medical preparation or medical treatment wherein the facilities and prisoners of any penal institution or inmates of any other institution in the State of Oklahoma are involved; and no such program shall hereafter be conducted in such institutions unless the particulars thereof have been previously approved by a majority of the Medical Research Commission and as to penal institutions also by the Department of Corrections.

§ 47.3   Contracts

The Medical Research Commission shall have authority to enter into contracts with companies, firms, or individuals for carrying on medical research projects or programs for the testing or experiment of any medical preparation or medical treatment in any of the institutions, including penal institutions, of the State of Oklahoma, providing such contract shall have, as to penal institutions, the prior approval of the Director of the Oklahoma Department of Corrections and, as to any other institution, shall have the prior approval of the governing board of the institution concerned.

§ 47.4   Gifts—Expenditures

The Medical Research Commission is authorized to accept contributions, grants, or gifts, from any private organization or individual, or any governmental agency or subdivision, for the promotion of medical research and is further authorized to enter into any contracts or agreements, which the Commission considers desirable, for the advancement of medical knowledge, and may match any funds which may be available from private or governmental sources with any funds the Commission may receive. All monies received by said Commission which were derived from a research program shall be deposited in the State Treasury to the credit of the Medical Research Commission which, after paying expenses of the research programs under its jurisdiction, shall deposit the remainder to the credit of the institution or department where the work was done. All monies expended from such account shall be controlled from the State Budget Office in the same manner as other state funds. All monies received from the plasmapheresis program at penal institutions shall be deposited in the State Treasury to the credit of the Department of Corrections. All expenditures incurred in the plasma program at penal institutions shall be paid by the Department of Corrections. Prices paid or credits issued to inmates of penal institutions who participate in any of these programs shall be set by the Director of the Department of Corrections.

§ 47.5 Delegation of execution of research programs

The Commission may delegate the execution of its research programs to physicians qualified in medical research, clinical investigation, experimental pharmacology and therapeutics or other medical specialty.

The following California statutory provision concerns research designed to facilitate early release from penal institutions. It is unusual in that it is concerned with research that relates specifically to their special status or interests as prisoners, rather than with their participation in research that could be conducted with other populations.

Cal. Penal Code §3049.5 (Supp. 1975) Prisoners included in specific research program approved by board of corrections

Notwithstanding the provisions of Section 3049, any prisoner selected for inclusion in a specific research program approved by the Board of Corrections may be paroled upon completion of the diagnostic study provided for in Section 5079. The number of prisoners released in any year under this provision shall not exceed 5 percent of the total number of all prisoners released in the preceding year.

This section shall not apply to a prisoner who, while committing the offense for which he has been imprisoned, physically attacked any person by any means. A threat of attack is not a physical attack for the purposes of this section unless such threat was accompanied by an attempt to inflict physical harm upon some person.

The Board of Corrections shall report to the Legislature on the fifth Legislative day of the 1974 Regular Session of the Legislature regarding any research program completed or in progress authorized under this section, and thereafter it shall report annually.

Innovative Therapy

There is a distinction between the performance of an experimental procedure and conducting a study involving an experimental use of a generally accepted procedure. When an experimental procedure is under consideration, particularly when its risks are substantial, public interest and concern about its use can be very high. Specific and detailed legislation often results.

A 1973 Oregon law regulating psychosurgery and intracranial brain stimulation is an example of a comprehensive regulatory plan with extensive procedures to deal with consent questions. Of particular interest are the definition of "experimental" in Section 426.700 and the membership of the Psychosurgery Review Board (set forth in Section 426.750), of which all but two are to be physicians or scientists. Note that Section 677.190 of the Oregon Revised Statutes provides that performing psychosurgery without permission of the Psychosurgery Review Board constitutes grounds for revocation of a physician's license by the medical licensing board.

Ore. Rev. Stat.
426.700   Definitions for ORS 426.700 to 426.755.

As used in ORS 426.700 to 426.755, unless the context requires otherwise:

(1) "Electro-convulsive therapy" means a nonsurgical and generalized electrical stimulation of the brain, designed to induce a convulsion.

(2) "Experimental" means a technique or procedure about which there is not sufficient data to recommend it as a recognized treatment of choice, or to predict accurately the outcome of its performance.

(3) "Intracranial brain stimulation" means the surgical implantation of electrodes within the brain for alteration stimulating specific brain structures to produce alteration of the thoughts, emotions, or behavior in a human being. Intracranial brain stimulation does not include electro-convulsive therapy.

(4) "Operation" means psychosurgery or intracranial brain stimulation.

(5) "Patient" means any person upon whom psychosurgery or intracranial brain stimulation is intended to be performed, including but not limited to persons confined voluntarily or involuntarily in any state institutions or private hospitals.

(6) "Psychosurgery" means any operation designed to irreversibly lesion or destroy brain tissue for the primary purpose of altering the thoughts, emotions or behavior of a human being. "Psychosurgery" does not include procedures which may irreversibly lesion or destroy brain tissues when undertaken to cure well-defined disease states such as brain tumor, epileptic foci and certain chronic pain syndromes.

(7) "Review board" means the Psychosurgery Review Board.

426.705 Psychosurgery and intracranial brain stimulation regulated.

No person, institution or hospital shall perform or cause to be performed psychosurgery or intracranial brain stimulation on any patient without complying with ORS 426.700 to 426.755 and 677.190.

426.710 Petition to perform surgery or stimulation; notice; hearing.

(1) Any institution, hospital or licensed physician intending to perform psychosurgery or intracranial brain stimulation for the primary purpose of altering the thoughts, emotions or behavior of a human being shall file a petition with the review board alleging that a patient is in need of such treatment, that the patient or his legal guardian, if any, has consented thereto, and that the proposed operation has legitimate clinical value.

(2) Within 10 days of the filing of the petition under subsection (1) of this section, the review board shall:

(a) Schedule a hearing to be held within 20 days to determine if the patient or his legal guardian has given his informed, voluntary consent.

(b) Give notice of the hearing at least seven days prior thereto to the patient, the legal guardian, if any, the legal counsel, if any, and the petitioner.

(c) Conduct the consent hearing.

426.715 Determination of voluntary and informed consent.

(1) At the hearing held pursuant to subsection (2) of ORS 426.710, the review board shall determine whether or not the patient or his legal guardian has given his voluntary and informed consent.

(2) For the review board to determine under subsection (1) of this section that the consent given was voluntary and

informed, it must appear that:

(a) A fair explanation was made of the procedures to be followed, including an identification of those which are experimental;

(b) A description was given of the attendant discomforts and risks, if any;

(c) A description was given of the benefits to be expected, if any;

(d) A disclosure was made of appropriate alternative treatments, if any, that would be advantageous for the subject;

(e) An offer was made to answer any inquiries concerning the treatment;

(f) Notice was given that the patient is free to withdraw his consent and to discontinue the authorized treatment at any time;

(g) Disclosure was made of the relationship between the patient and the institution, hospital or physician obtaining the consent; and

(h) Notice was given that the patient or his legal guardian, if any, had a right to consult with and be advised or represented by legal counsel, and if he could not afford one, legal counsel would be appointed for him pursuant to subsection (2) of ORS 426.735.

(3) If at any time during the hearing held under this section, the patient or his legal guardian requests an opportunity to consult or be represented by legal counsel, such a request shall be granted.

(4) At the conclusion of the hearing held under this section, the patient or his legal guardian, if any, shall be asked if he still consents to the proposed psychosurgery or intracranial brain stimulation.

(5) If the patient appears to be incapable of giving an informed and voluntary consent to the proposed operation, the necessary consent shall be required to be given or withheld by the patient's legal guardian.

426.720 Determination on clinical merit and appropriateness of operation.

(1) Subsequent to the hearing held under ORS 426.710, if the review board has found that the patient or his legal guardian has given his voluntary and informed consent to the

proposed operation the review board shall review the proposed operation and make a determination of whether or not the operation has clinical merit and is an appropriate treatment for the specific patient.

(2) In making its determination of whether or not the proposed operation has value in the specific clinical situation, the review board may study pertinent literature, reports and legislation, conduct consultations and interviews with persons knowledgeable in the field and conduct onsite visitations. In the event the review board determines that the proposed operation lacks clinical merit, the petition shall be denied and the petitioner notified by registered mail.

(3) If the review board finds that the proposed operation has legitimate clinical value, it shall review the clinical data of the patient proposed for the psychosurgery or intracranial brain stimulation operation. The review board shall determine whether or not such treatment is appropriate for the patient. In order for the review board to determine that such an operation is appropriate, it must appear that:

(a) All conventional therapies have been attempted;

(b) The criteria for selection of the patient have been met;

(c) The operation offers hope of saving life, reestablishing health or alleviating suffering; and

(d) All other viable alternative methods of treatment have been tried and have failed to produce satisfactory results.

(4) The review board may undertake a specific diagnostic evaluation as to the suitability of the patient for the proposed operation and the review board may establish the procedure for such evaluation.

(5) The review board shall make a written order embodying its conclusions. The order shall specify whether or not the psychosurgery or intracranial brain stimulation as requested in the petition may be performed.

(6) A copy of the order of the review board shall be served personally or by registered mail on:

(a) The petitioner;

(b) The patient;

(c) The legal guardian, if any; and

(d) The patient's or legal guardian's legal counsel, if any.

426.725 Oath; deposition; subpoena.

The review board may administer oaths, take depositions and issue subpoenas to compel the attendance of witnesses and the production of documents or other written information necessary to carry out the purposes of ORS 426.700 to 426.755 and 677.190. If any person fails to comply with a subpoena issued under this section or refuses to testify on matters on which he lawfully may be interrogated, the procedure set out in ORS 183.440 shall be followed to compel obedience.

426.730   Request for appointment of guardian; preference in appointment.

(1) If the patient does not have a legal guardian and the review board believes that the patient is incapable of giving an informed and voluntary consent to the proposed operation, the review board shall request that a legal guardian be appointed.

(2) Preference in appointment of a legal guardian under subsection (1) of this section shall be in the following order:

(a) The patient's spouse.

(b) The patient's nearest next of kin.

(c) A personal friend of the patient.

(d) A public guardian if one exists in the county, under the provisions of ORS 126.905 to 126.965.

(e) Any other person deemed appropriate by the court.

426.735   Representation by legal counsel; appointment; payment of fees.

(1) Any patient or legal guardian, if any, may be represented by legal counsel in the hearing held under ORS 426.715.

(2) If the patient or legal guardian requests to be represented by legal counsel but cannot afford one, the circuit court of the county in which the patient resides shall appoint:

(a) The county public defender to represent him, when the office of county public defender has been created under ORS 151.010 to 151.090.

(b) A member of the Oregon State Bar to represent him, when the office of the county public defender has not been created.

(3) The fee of the legal counsel appointed under paragraph (b) of subsection (2) of this section shall be paid out of funds appropriated by the county for the payment of appointed counsel.

426.740   Written report on operation required.

Upon completion of the psychosurgery or intracranial brain stimulation operation, the petitioner and any physician who performs the operation shall make a written report of their results to the review board.

426.745 Liability of board members and person performing operation; liability of institution or hospital.

(1) A member of the review board which permits psychosurgery or intracranial brain stimulation is presumed to be acting in good faith. Unless it is alleged and proved that his action violated the standard of reasonable professional care and judgment under the circumstances, he is immune from civil or criminal liability that otherwise might be incurred.

(2) A person who relies on the review board's permission to perform the psychosurgery or intracranial brain stimulation and performs such treatment is presumed to be acting in good faith. Unless it is alleged and proved that such person violated the standard of reasonable care and judgment under the circumstances, he is immune from civil or criminal liability that otherwise might be incurred.

(3) Any person, institution or hospital who performs psychosurgery or intracranial brain stimulation without obtaining permission of the Psychosurgery Review Board under ORS 426.705 to 426.740 and subsections (1) and (2) of this section shall be subject to civil liability for any damages which the patient suffers from the psychosurgery or intracranial brain stimulation.

426.750 Psychosurgery Review Board; term; vacancy; members.

(1) There is created the Psychosurgery Review Board consisting of nine persons appointed by the Governor.

(2) The term of office of each member is four years, but a member serves at the pleasure of the Governor. Before the expiration of the term of a member, the Governor shall appoint a successor whose term begins on July 1 next following. A member is eligible for reappointment. If there is a vacancy for any cause, the Governor shall make an appointment to become immediately effective for the unexpired term.

(3) Of the membership of the board:

(a) One shall be a physician licensed by the Board of Medical Examiners for the State of Oregon, practicing neurology, certified by the American Board of Neurology and Psychiatry, and nominated pursuant to ORS 426.755;

(b) Two shall be physicians licensed by the Board of Medical Examiners for the State of Oregon, practicing neurosurgery, certified by the American Board of Neurosurgery, and nominated pursuant to ORS 426.755;

(c) Two shall be physicians licensed by the Board of Medical Examiners for the State of Oregon, practicing psychiatry, certified by the American Board of Neurology and Psychiatry, and nominated pursuant to ORS 426.755;

(d) One shall be a clinical psychologist;

(e) One shall be a neuroscientist actively engaged in research on the nervous system; and

(f) Two shall be members of the general public one of whom shall be a member of the Oregon State Bar.

(4) All decisions of the review board shall be made by the affirmative vote of not less than six members.

(5) No individual directly involved in conducting psychosurgery or intracranial brain stimulation on human beings shall be a member of the review board.

426.755   Nomination of members.

Not later than June 1 of each year, the Oregon Medical Association shall nominate three qualified physicians for each physician member of the Psychosurgery Review Board whose term expires in that year, and shall certify its nominees to the Governor. The Governor shall consider these nominees in selecting successors to retiring board members.

677.190   Grounds for suspension or revocation of license.

The board may suspend or revoke a license to practice medicine in this state for any of the following reasons:

*   *   *

(23) Performing psychosurgery or intracranial brain stimulation without obtaining permission of the Psychosurgery Review Board under ORS 426.705 to 426.740, subsections (1) and (2) of 426.745, ORS 426.750 and 426.755.

California's 1974 legislation dealing with "organic therapy," including psychosurgery, shock therapy, and the use of drugs and other agents or techniques in programs of aversive and other types of conditioning applies only to persons confined involuntarily. It limits the use of psychosurgery solely to such persons who can and do give "informed consent" and provides a court procedure for determining issues related to consent to, and benefits to be derived from, organic therapy. The legislation, which follows, specifically provides in section 2680 that, when the attending physician decides organic therapy should be administered to a person, such person shall be given a copy of the legislation to ensure that he understands his rights under it.

Cal. Penal Code (Supp. 1975)

§ 2670   Declaration of policy

It is hereby recognized and declared that all persons, including all persons involuntarily confined, have a fundamental right against enforced interference with their thought processes, states of mind, and patterns of mentation through the use of organic therapies; that this fundamental right requires that no person with the capacity for informed consent who refuses organic therapy shall be compelled to undergo such therapy; and that in order to justify the use of organic therapy upon a person who lacks the capacity for informed consent, other than psychosurgery as referred to in subdivision (c) of Section 2670.5 which is not to be administered to such persons, the state shall establish that the organic therapy would be beneficial to the person, that there is a compelling interest in administering such therapy, and that there are no less onerous alternatives to such therapy.

§ 2670.5   Informed consent to organic thereapy; persons lacking capacity; organic therapy defined; withdrawal of consent.

(a) No person confined or detained under Title 1 (commencing with Section 2000) and Title 2 (commencing with Section 3200) shall be administered or subjected to any organic therapy as defined in subdivision (c) without his informed consent, provided that:

(1) If the person gives his informed consent to organic therapy, it shall be administered only if there has been compliance with Sections 2675 through 2680, inclusive.

(2) If the person lacks the capacity for informed consent to organic therapy other than psychosurgery as referred to in subdivision (c), in order to proceed with such therapy, the warden or superintendent shall secure an order from the superior court to authorize the administration of such therapy in accordance with Sections 2675 through 2680.

(b) No person confined or detained under Title 1 (commencing with Section 2000) or Title 2 (commencing with Section 3200) who lacks the capacity for informed consent shall be administered or subjected to psychosurgery as referred to in subdivision (c).

(c) The term organic therapy refers to:

(1) Psychosurgery, including lobotomy, stereotactic surgery, electronic, chemical or other destruction of brain tissues, or implantation of electrodes into brain tissue.

(2) Shock therapy, including but not limited to any convulsive therapy and insulin shock treatments.

(3) The use of any drugs, electric shocks, electronic stimulation of the brain, or infliction of physical pain when used as an aversive or reinforcing stimulus in a program of aversive, classical, or operant conditioning.

(d) A person does not waive his right to refuse any organic therapy by having previously given his informed consent to such therapy, and he may withdraw his consent at any time.

If required by sound medical-psychiatric practice, the attending physician shall, after the person withdraws his previously given informed consent, gradually phase the person out of the therapy if sudden cessation would create a serious risk of mental or physical harm to the person.

(e) Nothing in this article shall be construed to prevent the attending physician from administering nonorganic therapies such as psychotherapy, psychoanalysis, group therapy, milieu therapy, or other therapies or programs involving communication or interaction among physicians, patients, and others, with or without the use of drugs when used for purposes other than described in paragraph (3) of subdivision (c).

(f) Nothing in this article shall be construed to prevent the administration of drugs not connected with a program of conditioning and intended to cause negative physical reactions to ingestion of alcohol or drugs.

§ 2671   Persons inflicting or attempting to inflict substantial physical harm upon themselves or others; shock therapy consent

(a) Notwithstanding Section 2670.5, if a confined person has inflicted or attempted to inflict substantial physical harm upon the person of another or himself, or presents, as a result of mental disorder, an imminent threat of substantial harm to others or himself, the attending physician may in such emergency employ or authorize for no longer than seven days in any three-month period the immediate use of shock treatments in order to alleviate such danger.

(b) Notwithstanding Section 2670.5, if a confined person gives his informed consent to a program of shock therapy for a period not to exceed three months, the attending physician may administer such therapy for a period not to exceed three

months in any one-year period without prior judicial authorization.

§ 2672 Informed consent; capacity

(a) For purposes of this article, "informed consent" means
that a person must knowingly and intelligently, without
duress or coercion, and clearly and explicitly manifest his
consent to the proposed organic therapy to the attending
physician.

(b) A person confined shall not be deemed incapable of
informed consent solely by virtue of being diagnosed as a
mentally ill, disordered, abnormal or mentally defective person.

(c) A person confined shall be deemed incapable of informed consent if such person cannot understand, or knowingly and intelligently act upon, the information specified in
Section 2673.

(d) A person confined shall be deemed incapable of informed consent if for any reason he cannot manifest his
consent to the attending physician.

§ 2673 Information required prior to an informed consent

(a) For purposes of this article, "informed consent" requires that the attending physician directly communicate
with the person and clearly and explicitly provide all the
following information prior to the person's decision:

(1) The nautre and seriousness of the person's illness,
disorder or defect.

(2) The nature of the proposed organic therapy and its
intended duration.

(3) The likelihood of improvement or deterioration, tempo-
rary or permanent, without the administration of the proposed organic therapy.

(4) The likelihood and degree of improvement, remission,
control, or cure resulting from the administration of such
organic therapy, and the likelihood, nature, and extent of
changes in and intrusions upon the person's personality and
patterns of behavior and thought or mentation and the
degree to which these changes may be irreversible. This
information shall indicate the probable duration and in-
tensity of such therapy and whether such therapy may have
to be continued indefinitely for optimum therapeutic benefit.

(5) The likelihood, nature, extent, and duration of side effects of the proposed organic therapy, and how and to what extent they may be controlled, if at all.

(6) The uncertainty of the benefits and hazards of the proposed organic therapy because of the lack of sufficient data available to the medical profession, or any other reason for such uncertainty.

(7) The reasonable alternative organic therapy or psychotherapeutic modality of therapy, or nonorganic behavior modification programs, and why the organic therapy recommended is the therapy of choice. These alternatives shall be described and explained to the person in the manner specified in this section.

(8) Whether the proposed therapy is generally regarded as sound by the medical profession, or is considered experimental.

§ 2674   Written consent required

A written manifestation of informed consent shall be obtained in all cases by the attending physician and shall be preserved and available to the person, his attorney, his guardian, or his conservator.

§ 2675   Petition to superior court; order authorizing treatment; responsive pleadings

(a) If the proposed organic therapy is not prohibited by subdivision (a) or (b) of Section 2670.5, then in order to administer such therapy the warden or superintendent of the institution in which the person is confined shall petition the superior court of the county in which the person is confined for an order authorizing such organic therapy.

(b) The petition shall summarize the facts which the attending physician is required to communicate to the person pursuant to Section 2673, and shall state whether the person has the capacity for informed consent, and, if so, whether the person has given his informed consent to the proposed therapy. The petition shall clearly specify what organic therapy the institution proposes to administer to the person. The petition shall specify what mental illness, disorder, abnormality, or defect justifies the administration of such therapy. Copies of the petition shall be personally served upon the person and served upon his attorney, guardian or conservator on the same day as it is filed with the clerk of the superior court.

(c) The person confined, or his attorney, guardian or conservator may file a response to such petition for organic therapy. Said response shall be filed no later than 10 days after service of the said petition unless the court grants a continuance not to exceed 10 additional days, and shall be served on the warden or superintendent on the same day it is filed.

§ 2676   Petition to superior court; order prohibiting administration of organic therapy; responsive pleadings

(a) Any person, or his attorney, guardian or conservator may file a petition with the superior court of the county in which he is confined for an order to prohibit the administration upon him of an organic therapy. The filing of such a petition shall constitute a refusal of consent or withdrawal of any prior consent to an organic therapy. The clerk of the court shall serve a copy of such petition, on the same day it is filed, upon the warden or superintendent.

(b) The warden or superintendent shall file a response to such petition to prohibit the enforced administration of any organic therapy. Such response shall be filed no later than 10 days after the filing of the petition, unless the court grants a continuance not to exceed 10 additional days, and shall be personally served upon the person and served upon his attorney, guardian or conservator on the same day as it is filed with the clerk of the superior court. Such response shall not constitute a petition for an order to proceed with any organic therapy pursuant to Section 2675, which shall be the exclusive procedure for authorization to administer any organic therapy.

§ 2677   Appointment medical expert

At the time of filing of a petition pursuant to Section 2676 by the person, or pursuant to Section 2675 by the warden or superintendent, the court shall appoint the public defender or other attorney to represent the person unless the person is financially able to provide his own attorney. The attorney shall advise the person of his rights in relation to the proceeding in question and shall represent him before the court.

The court shall also appoint an independent medical expert on the person's behalf to examine the person's medical, mental, or emotional condition and to testify thereon, unless the person is financially able to obtain such expert testimony; provided that, if the person has given his informed consent to the proposed organic therapy, other than psychosurgery as referred to in subdivision (c) of Section 2670.5, and his attorney concurs in the proposed administration of such organic therapy, the court may waive the requirement that such an independent medical expert be appointed.

§ 2678   Proceedings on petition; continuance

The court shall conduct the proceedings within 10 judicial days from the filing of the petition described in Section 2675 or 2676, whichever is filed earlier, unless the warden or superintendent's attorney or the person's attorney requests a continuance, which may be for a maximum of 10 additional judicial days.   The court shall conduct the proceedings in accordance with constitutional guarantees of due process of law and the procedures under Section 13 of Article I of the California Constitution.

§ 2679   Determination by court

(a) The court shall determine whether the state has proven, by clear and convincing evidence, that the confined person has the capacity for informed consent and has manifested his informed consent.

(b) If the court has determined that the person lacks the capacity for informed consent, the court shall determine by clear and convincing evidence that such therapy, other than psychosurgery as referred to in subdivision (c) of Section 2670.5, would be beneficial; that there is a compelling interest justifying the use of the organic therapy upon the person; that there are no less onerous alternatives to such organic therapy; and that such organic therapy is in accordance with sound medical-psychiatric practice.   If the court so determines, then the court shall authorize the administration of the organic therapy for a period not to exceed six months.

(c) If the court has determined that the person has the capacity for informed consent and has manifested his informed consent to organic therapy, the court shall determine by clear and convincing evidence that such therapy would be beneficial; that there is a compelling interest justifying the use of the organic therapy upon the person; that there are no less onerous alternatives to such organic therapy; and that such organic therapy is in accordance with sound medical-psychiatric practice. If the court so determines then the court shall authorize the administration of the organic therapy for a period not to exceed six months.

§2680   Advice and information of rights; application of article; communications regarding proposed administration of organic therapy; termination of therapy prior to authorized period

(a) If it is determined by the attending physician that a confined person should be administered organic therapy, such person shall be advised and informed of his rights under this article, and he shall be provided a copy of this article.

(b) All provisions of this article shall apply to prisoners confined under the provisions of this part in public or private hospitals, sanitariums, and similar facilities, and to the personnel of such facilities.

(c) A person shall be entitled to communicate in writing and by visiting with his parents, guardian, or conservator regarding any proposed administration of any organic therapy. Such communication shall not be censored. Such person shall be entitled to communicate in writing with his attorney pursuant to Section 2600 of the Penal Code.

(d) Nothing in this article shall prohibit the attending physician from terminating organic therapy prior to the period authorized for such therapy by the court, pursuant to Section 2679.

Confidentiality of Information and Privacy

Many statutory provisions pertaining to research involving human subjects contain language concerning the maintenance of confidentiality. Some of the excerpts already included in this chapter contain such language. The purpose of confidentiality requirements is to protect the privacy of the individuals with whom the data are concerned.

A California provision requires, in the statute excerpted below, that researchers sign a written "oath of confidentiality" before they can be granted access to information and records obtained in the course of providing mental health services. In the oath the researcher agrees not to divulge information to unauthorized persons or to publish data that identify individuals.

*   *   *

Cal. Welf. & Inst. Code §5328 (Supp. 1975) Confidential information and records; disclosure

All information and records obtained in the course of providing services under Division 5 (commencing with Section 5000), Division 6 (commencing with Section 6000), or Division 7 (commencing with Section 7000), to either voluntary or involuntary recipients of services shall be confidential. Information and records may be disclosed only:

*   *   *

(e) For research, provided that the Director of Health designates by regulation, rules for the conduct of research. Such rules shall include, but need not be limited to, the requirement that all researchers must sign an oath of confidentiality as follows:

——————————

Date

As a condition of doing research concerning persons who have received services from —————— (fill in the facility, agency or person), I, ——————, agree not to divulge any information obtained in the course of such research to unauthorized persons, and not to publish or otherwise make public any information regarding persons who have received services such that the person who received services is identifiable.

I recognize that unauthorized release of confidential information may make me subject to a civil action under provisions of the Welfare and Institutions Code.

——————————

Signed

The confidentiality of reports and records of medical care studies is covered in the legislation of many states. Illinois specifically forbids interviews with patients named in such studies and their relatives and friends without prior consent of the attending physician.

Ill. Ann. Stat., Ch. 51 (1966)
§ 101   Information obtained—Confidential nature

All information, interviews, reports, statements, memoranda or other data of the Illinois Department of Public Health, Illinois State Medical Society, allied medical societies, or in-hospital staff committees of accredited hospitals, but not the original medical records pertaining to the patient, used in the course of medical study for the purpose of reducing morbidity or mortality shall be strictly confidential and shall be used only for medical research.

§ 102 Admissibility as evidence—Prohibition
Such information, records, reports, statements, notes, memoranda, or other data, shall not be admissible as evidence in any action of any kind in any court or before any tribunal, board, agency or person.

§ 103 Furnishing information in course of research project—Immunity from liability
The furnishing of such information in the course of a research project to the Illinois Department of Public Health, Illinois State Medical Society, allied medical societies or to in-hospital staff committees or their authorized representatives, shall not subject any person, hospital, sanitarium, nursing or rest home or any such agency to any action for damages or other relief.

§ 104 Interviews—Consent of physician
No patient, patient's relatives, or patient's friends named in any medical study, shall be interviewed for the purpose of such study unless consent of the attending physician and surgeon is first obtained.

Ill. Ann. Stat., Ch. 51 (Supp. 1975)
§ 105 Improper disclosure of information—Penalty
The disclosure of any information, records, reports, statements, notes, memoranda or other data obtained in any such medical study except that necessary for the purpose of the specific study is unlawful, and any person convicted of violating any of the provisions of this Act is guilty of a Class A misdemeanor.

Declarations of Patient's Rights

State governmental concern regarding research with human subjects can be manifested in legislation or regulations concerning rights of patients in regulated health services institutions. The attention to rights of patients has increased during the 1970s; and in some states it has been manifested in legislation or regulations, which either establish a "Bill of Rights" for patients in regulated institutions or require such institutions to do so. Among the subjects usually mentioned in such documents are the right of the patient to be informed about his possible involvement in research and the requirement of informed consent prior to participation. These statements emphasize the trend toward greater public concern about individual rights in the process of securing subjects for research. An excerpt from the New York Hospital Code illustrates a "Patient's Bill of Rights" containing such a reference to experimentation.

N.Y.C.R.R. §720.3 Patients' Rights

(a) The hospital shall establish written policies regarding the rights of patients and shall develop procedures implementing such policies. These rights, policies, and procedures shall afford patients the right to:

*   *   *

(5) receive from his physician information necessary to give informed consent prior to the start of any procedure or treatment or both and which, except for those emergency situations not requiring an informed consent, shall include as a minimum the specific procedure or treatment or both, the medically significant risks involved, and the probable duration of incapacitation, if any. The patient shall be advised of medically significant alternatives for care or treatment if any,

*   *   *

(12) refuse to participate in research and that human experimentation affecting care or treatment shall be performed only with his informed effective consent,

*   *   *

(b) A copy of the provisions of this section shall be available to each patient or patient's representatives upon admission and posted in conspicuous places within the hospital.

Comprehensive Review of Human Research

Drawing to a considerable extent on the DHEW regulations, New York enacted a statute applying to all human research, which is defined to include any experiment or investigation involving human subjects that involves physical or psychological intervention on a subject's body not required for preventive, diagnostic, or therapeutic purposes for the direct benefit of the subject. The statute contains a detailed description of informed consent and requires institutions to establish human research review committees. The statute does not apply to human research subject to and in compliance with policies and regulations for the protection of human subjects of a federal agency; thus, this legislation would not ordinarily apply to research conducted with DHEW financial support.

N.Y. Pub. Health Law §§ 2440-2446 (Supp. 1976).

§ 2440   Policy and purpose

The use of human subjects in medical research projects has brought about many beneficial scientific advances resulting in the increased health and well-being of the human race. Safeguarding the rights and welfare of individual human subjects in the conduct of these human research projects is a matter of vital state concern. Every human being has the right to be protected against the possible conduct of medical or psychological research upon his body without his voluntary informed consent. Human research may effect dangerous and unanticipated results causing irreversible damage to the human subject. Accordingly, it shall be the policy of this state to protect its people against the unnecessary and improper risk of pain, suffering or injury resulting from human research conducted without their knowledge or consent.

§ 2441   Definitions

For the purpose of this article: 1. "Human subject" shall mean any individual who may be exposed to the possibility of injury, including physical, psychological or social injury, as a consequence of participation as a subject in any research, development, or related activity which departs from the application of those established and accepted methods necessary to meet his needs or which increases the ordinary risk of daily life including the recognized risks inherent in a chosen occupation or field of service.

2. "Human research" means any medical experiments, research, or scientific or psychological investigation, which utilizes human subjects and which involves physical or psychological intervention by the researcher upon the body of the subject and which is not required for the purposes of obtaining information for the diagnosis, prevention, or treatment of disease or the assessment of medical condition for the direct benefit of the subject. Human research shall not, however, be construed to mean the conduct of biological

studies exclusively utilizing tissue or fluids after their removal or withdrawal from a human subject in the course of standard medical practice, or to include epidemiological investigations.

3. "Fluid" means a normal body excretion or any fluid formed by normal or pathological body processes obtained during diagnostic or therapeutic procedures conducted for the benefit of the human subject.

4. "Tissue" means part or all of any organ of a human subject removed during a diagnostic or therapeutic procedure conducted for the benefit of the human subject.

5. "Voluntary informed consent" means the legally effective knowing consent of an individual or his legally authorized representative, so situated as to be able to exercise free power of choice without undue inducement or any element of force, fraud, deceit, duress or other form of constraint or coercion. With regard to the conduct of human research, the basic elements of information necessary to such consent include:

(a) a fair explanation to the individual of the procedures to be followed, and their purposes, including identification of any procedures which are experimental;

(b) a description of any attendant discomforts and risks reasonably to be expected;

(c) a description of any benefits reasonably to be expected;

(d) a disclosure of any appropriate alternative procedures that might be advantageous for the individual;

(e) an offer to answer any inquiries by the individual concerning the procedures; and

(f) an instruction that the individual is free to withdraw his consent and to discontinue participation in the human research at any time without prejudice to him.

6. "Researcher" means any person licensed under title VIII of the education law to perform diagnosis, treatment, medical services, prescription or therapeutic exercises with regard to or upon human beings, or any other person deemed appropriately competent and qualified by a human research review committee as provided by section twenty-four hundred forty-four of this chapter.

§ 2442   Informed consent

No human research may be conducted in this state in the absence of the voluntary informed consent subscribed to in writing by the human subject. If the human subject be a minor, such consent shall be subscribed to in writing by the minor's parent or legal guardian. If the human subject be otherwise legally unable to render consent, such consent shall be subscribed to in writing by such other person as may be legally empowered to act on behalf of the human subject. No such voluntary informed consent shall include any language through which the human subject waives, or appears to waive, any of his legal rights, including any release of any individual, institution or agency, or any agents thereof, from liability for negligence.

§ 2443 Conduct of human research
No one except a researcher shall conduct human research in this state.

§ 2444 Human research review committees
1.   Each public or private institution or agency which conducts, or which proposes to conduct or authorize, human research, shall establish a human research review committee. Such committee shall be composed of not less than five persons, approved by the commissioner, who have such varied backgrounds as to assure the competent, complete and professional review of human research activities conducted or proposed to be conducted or authorized by the institution or agency. No member of a committee shall be involved in either the initial or continuing review of an activity in which he has a conflicting interest, except to provide information required by the committee. No committee shall consist entirely of persons who are officers, employees, or agents of, or who are otherwise associated with the institution or agency, apart from their membership on the committee, and no committee shall consist entirely of members of a single professional group.
2.   The human research review committee in each institution or agency shall require that institution or agency to promulgate a statement of principle and policy in regard to the rights and welfare of human subjects in the conduct of human research, and the committee and the commissioner shall approve that statement prior to its taking effect. The committee shall review each proposed human research project to determine (1) its necessity; (2) that the rights and welfare of the human subjects involved are adequately pro-

tected; (3) that the risks to the human subjects are out-weighed by the potential benefits to them or by the importance of the knowledge to be gained; (4) that the voluntary informed consent is to be obtained by methods that are adequate and appropriate, and (5) that the persons proposed to conduct the particular medical research are appropriately competent and qualified. The committee shall periodically examine each existing human research project with regard to the proper application of the approved principles and policies which the institution or agency has promulgated. The committee shall report any violation to the commissioner. In addition to the voluntary informed consent of the proposed human subject as required by section twenty-four hundred forty-two of this chapter, the consent of the committee and the commissioner shall be required with relation to the conduct of human research involving minors, incompetent persons, mentally disabled persons and prisoners.

3. Each person engaged in the conduct of human research or proposing to conduct human research shall affiliate himself with an institution or agency having a human research review committee, and such human research as he conducts or proposes to conduct shall be subject to review by such committee in the manner set forth in this section.

§ 2445   Applicability

The provisions of this article shall not apply to the conduct of human research which is subject to, and which is in compliance with, policies and regulations promulgated by any agency of the federal government for the protection of human subjects.

§ 2446   Rules and regulations

The commissioner shall have the power to promulgate such rules and regulations as shall be necessary and proper to effectuate the purposes of this article.

OTHER LEGAL CONSIDERATIONS

A considerable number of legal concepts and principles could, depending on the circumstances, come into play and cause problems for investigators and institutions involved in research with human subjects. If the procedures suggested for institutional review in the preceding chapters are established and followed, the likelihood of any serious difficulties on these grounds seems remote.

Mention of these concepts and principles is to alert those involved in research. Two relate to children: child abuse and determinations that children are dependent or neglected. Although the law recognizes considerable latitude in the authority and responsibility that parents may exercise, under certain circumstances a parent's consent to his child's participation in a research study could lead to criminal liability for child abuse for both the parent and the investigator. The criminal liability risk for abuse of the child would be present only where harm clearly was inflicted on the child as part of the study. The parents in such a situation could also be found to have failed so seriously to meet their responsibilities that a court could find the children "dependent and neglected" under state law and place them in the custody of an individual or organization to protect their interests.

Another set of concepts relates to the potential for civil liability if confidentiality procedures are not followed or are intentionally violated. Safeguards exist, such as maintaining locked files and removing names and other identifying information from records of interviews or examinations. Should unauthorized persons secure access to the information, because safeguards were not employed or were carelessly followed, a basis for liability for harm to reputation or injury to feelings and sensibilities from disclosure would exist. The liability risk would be even more clear where if confidential information (according to the protocol) were furnished to unauthorized persons. Depending on the nature of the unprotected information or record and the use made of it, liability could be imposed for defamation (libel or slander), where the information was not accurate; for invasion of privacy; or for breach of the developing concept of confidentiality, predicated in part on professional licensure requirements and professional ethics, to which the person disclosing or making available the information is subject. The extent of liability would depend on the harm suffered by the individual concerned as the result of such wrongful conduct.

This risk of civil liability is separate from sanctions imposed by law where information was disclosed contrary to requirements for confidentiality present in applicable statutes or regulations. However, the failure to adhere to such requirements, in addition to resulting in such sanctions, could also lay a basis for civil liability to the individuals the disclosed information concerned, where they were able to establish harm to their personal interest.

Two additional points concerning confidentiality need mention. First, failure to adhere to confidentiality procedures in the protocol would be found by a court to constitute either negligence or intentional wrongful conduct. The fact that the institutional review board had approved the protocol only after confidentiality had been assured and assurances given to subjects before they consented to participate would influence a court considerably. Second, when a situation arises where the investigator believes, because of potential benefits to the subjects or for other purposes, that information he has acquired concerning subjects should be disclosed to persons to whom the subjects have not yet authorized disclosure, the opportunity exists to solicit and secure their consent specifically to such disclosure. Consent obtained from the subjects for disclosure of the information would eliminate risks of civil liability under the concepts and principles discussed earlier.

Court decisions, in greater number in the past two decades than before, have been concerned with issues relating to recognition and protection of personal rights. Particularly affected have been activities and practices relating to various categories of persons such as students, the mentally ill, and prisoners, all of whom are particularly subject to institutional pressures. Litigation in which these issues have been raised often has been based on allegations that federally protected rights have been interfered with by the state or by individuals acting in concert with or on behalf of the state. Of pertinence to the conduct of research with prisoner subjects is the decision in *Mackey v. Procunier*, 477 F.2d 877 (9th Cir. 1973). The appellate court here considered whether the allegation of experimentation with drugs for aversive therapy without the prisoner's consent to participation in that experiment raised constitutional issues, particularly, whether it could constitute "cruel and unusual punishment" under the Eighth Amendment to the United States Constitution. The Ninth Circuit Court of Appeals, in reversing the lower court by vacating its order to dismiss the prisoner's suit, indicated that serious constitutional questions would be present if the allegations were proved.

Even if the issue of whether consent to aversive therapy can be withdrawn at any time by someone who is undergoing such discomforting therapy is put aside, the questions of informed consent to, and withdrawal from, similar experiments on prisoners are serious and complicated. The court in the *Mackey* case appeared willing to accept the argument that, when drugs are used for conditions other than those for which they are intended and accepted in medical practice, they can be considered "experimental." Relevant to whether the drugs are used in such a manner is the content of the labeling information. Thus, use of a drug for a condition other than those stated in the labeling information accompanying the drug could raise the experimentation issue and, if used without informed consent, could provide a basis for a court to find liability.

Finally, some attention must be directed to liability for negligence or malpractice in the conduct of a study involving human subjects. As would be true in rendering services in a purely therapeutic setting, failure to provide services in a manner consistent with the generally accepted standard of performance could lead to liability for harm resulting from such failure. Thus, the liability risk attending inserting a catheter would be the same, regardless of whether this recognized procedure was performed as part of a study or in a routine therapeutic care context.

The liability risk arising from the performance of experimental procedures, or the performance of accepted procedures for experimental purposes, is more difficult to ascertain. Mention was made in Chapter 1 of several court decisions indicating that the "experimenter" is responsible for harm that results from his procedures. One difficulty facing the innovator in this context, is that the court might be inclined to follow the strong language of the early decisions. Where the procedure itself is experimental, the risk of liability would appear great, assuming that the harm suffered by the subject can be shown to be caused by the procedure. The subject would have to establish the causal relationship between the procedure and the harm suffered. This could prove difficult where the condition of the subject was such that recognized therapeutic interventions offered little chance for success and the harm alleged was the failure to arrest the progress of the condition or to effect repair of a damaged organ or limb, which could not be repaired by conventional therapy.

The decision in *Karp v. Cooley*, 493 F.2d 408 (1974), may be of solace to investigators. The court here found that the patient had been adequately informed about, and given consent to, the use of a mechanical heart, and ruled that there was no liability for the use of the device, which had never before been employed in a human.

In a situation where a recognized procedure or therapeutic agent is used in an innovative manner, the standard against which performance is measured in a malpractice action is unclear. The decision to adopt the innovative approach can be viewed as an exercise of sound clinical judgment when conventional therapeutic approaches either have been attempted and have failed or are contraindicated. In this context, as well as where an experimental procedure is used, the subject would have to establish that the harm allegedly suffered was caused by the innovative therapeutic activity, in addition to establishing a departure from the relevant standard of care.

When a controlled study in progress strongly indicates that the innovative therapy is far superior to the conventional one, and the study is continued for its planned duration, a serious risk of liability should be recognized. Present here is the possibility of a conflict between rigid adherence to a protocol and proper exercise of clinical judgment. In this situation the argument can be made that, once sufficient data were obtained to support the hypothesis, continuing to provide the conventional therapy to the controls in the study is contrary to scientific principles and constitutes a breach of duty (in that more effective therapy is being withheld to their detriment). The argument is similar to the one that can be made where a controlled study in progress strongly indicates that innovative therapy is unsuccessful, is causing substantially more harm, and is continued nevertheless. In either circumstance, continuation of the study could be viewed as malpractice on the part of the investigator.

At some point in a controlled study, information might be obtained that, after evaluation, strongly indicates new parameters of risk. Prospective subjects are entitled, as part of the information provided to them, to be informed of the current assessment of risks when their consent to participation is solicited. This might entail changes in the consent form used in the study. It would appear that the concept of informed consent is violated when such information is withheld and that continuation of a study under such circumstances (without providing information material to the exercise of decision making by prospective subjects) involves risks of liability. If the prospective subjects are informed of the risks then apparent and decide, nevertheless, to participate, and continuation of the study is considered to be in accord with standards of investigators, the liability risks on both informed consent and malpractice theories would be diminished, if not obviated.

Essentially the same disclosure requirement applies to subjects who have not completed their participation. They should be informed of the changed assessment of risks based on information unavailable when their consent to participate was secured, so they are able to decide whether to withdraw from, or to continue in, the study.

SOME FINAL OBSERVATIONS

Looking to the future, there are some observations concerning the direction of the law affecting research with human subjects the authors would like to make.

We anticipate increasing state regulatory activity. As the federal government and a few pioneer states provide clearer models, other states are likely to follow in the same manner as legislation providing for professional licensure and state food and drug laws swept the country. It is unlikely that many states will permit their citizens to be afforded little protection in the research context, other than by the threat of suit for liability on tort theories, merely because the research is not federally funded.

State common law has provided the underlying minimum legal constraints on research through tort liability and, in particular, through professional liability. However, the increasing cost and the decreasing availability of professional liability insurance has led to a variety of legislative efforts that affect the standards professionals are expected to meet and the processes by which the determination is made whether the standard has been met in a particular instance. There is a developing interest in a system to provide compensation without the need to establish fault. Any such change in the law of professional liability will have an affect on the scope and nature of the liability of clinical investigators, other researchers, and their institutions because of the extent to which the activities performed as part of investigations are considered professional conduct subject to such standards.

There have been as yet only sporadic investigations of the effectiveness of procedures required in the regulation of research, procedures such as: (1) to avoid taking advantages of certain classes of subjects and (2) to determine the extent that prospective subjects comprehend the information provided to them prior to their giving consent. We should anticipate increased investigations into the conduct of research itself to determine whether the rules, principles, and practices under which the research is conducted are effective in achieving their intended purposes. Such studies may effect the direction in which regulations develop.

Steps taken to protect human subjects can increase the time, effort, and financial undertaking necessary to carry out research endeavors. It remains to be seen how deep the commitment to the protection of subjects will be, when it must be balanced with competing societal interests, particularly where adherence to procedures for protection of human subjects substantially increases the costs of research. For example, if the use of prisoners in drug research reduces the cost much below the expense when subjects are obtained from the general population, will there be pressure to continue to utilize prisoners, even when it is recognized that they may well be subject to subtle coercion because of the nature or their environment? This conflict of values or interests is emphasized as the awareness grows that resources are finite and the difficult questions of allocation must be faced.

There is increasing public and political scrutiny of the research enterprise. Greater awareness of research and the impact of its results on everyday life is manifest. For many types of medical research, this leads to action by funding agencies to encourage investigators to concentrate on research with the potential for immediate applications. For other types of research, there is pressure to prohibit, or at least limit, research in an effort to avoid the major societal changes that it might cause. The whole process of allocating research funds is being scrutinized. Changes in the process could have a substantial impact on the nature of research that will be conducted.

The National Commission for the Protection of Human Subjects of Biomedical and Behavioral Research will be a significant force in determining the directions that new governmental regulations concerning research will take. Its existence emphasizes the public scrutiny that research is receiving. It also exemplifies the effort to introduce people with a wide variety of points of view into the process of formulating the rules that will govern research with human subjects.

APPENDIX A SELECTED PROFESSIONAL CODES AND GUIDELINES

MEDICAL

Declaration of Helsinki, 1964
World Medical Association

It is the mission of the doctor to safeguard the health of the people. His knowledge and conscience are dedicated to the fulfilment of this mission.

The Declaration of Geneva of the World Medical Association (1964) binds the doctor with the words, "The health of my patient will be my first consideration"; and the International Code of Medical Ethics which declares that "Any act or advice which could weaken physical or mental resistance of a human being may be used only in his interest."

Because it is essential that the results of laboratory experiments be applied to human beings to further scientific knowledge and to help suffering humanity, the World Medical Association has prepared the following recommendations as a guide to each doctor in clinical research. It must be stressed that the standards as drafted are only a guide to physicians all over the world. Doctors are not relieved from criminal, civil, and ethical responsibilities under the laws of their own countries.

In the field of clinical research a fundamental distinction must be recognized between clinical research in which the aim is essentially therapeutic for a patient, and clinical research the essential object of which is purely scientific and without therapeutic value to the person subjected to the research.

I. Basic Principles

1. Clinical research must conform to the moral and scientific principles that justify medical research, and should be based on laboratory and animal experiments or other scientifically established facts. [The use of animals is not always feasible or possible.]

2. Clinical research should be conducted only by scientifically qualified persons and under the supervision of a qualified medical man.

3. Clinical research cannot legitimately be carried out unless the importance of the objective is in proportion to the inherent risk to the subject.

4. Every clinical research project should be preceded by careful assessment of inherent risks in comparison to foreseeable benefits to the subject or to others.

5. Special caution should be exercised by the doctor in performing clinical research in which the personality of the subject is liable to be altered by drugs or experimental procedure.

II. Clinical Research Combined with Professional Care

1. In the treatment of the sick person the doctor must be free to use a new therapeutic measure, if in his judgment it offers hope of saving life, re-establishing health, or alleviating suffering.

If at all possible, consistent with patient psychology, the doctor should obtain the patient's freely given consent after the patient has been given full explanation. In case of legal incapacity consent should also be procured from the legal guardian; in case of physical incapacity the permission of the legal guardian replaces that of the patient.

2. The doctor can combine clinical research with professional care, the objective being the acquisition of new medical knowledge, only to the extent that clinical research is justified by its therapeutic value for the patient.

III. Non-therapeutic Clinical Research

1. In the purely scientific application of clinical research carried out on a human being it is the duty of the doctor to remain the protector of the life and health of that person on whom clinical research is being carried out.

2. The nature, the purpose, and the risk of clinical research must be explained to the subject by the doctor.

3a. Clinical research on a human being cannot be undertaken without his free consent, after he has been fully informed; if he is legally incompetent the consent of the legal guardian should be procured.

3b. The subject of clinical research should be in such a mental, physical, and legal state as to be able to exercise fully his power of choice.

3c. Consent should as a rule be obtained in writing. However, the responsibility for clinical research always remains with the research worker; it never falls on the subject, even after consent is obtained.

4a. The investigator must respect the right of each individual to safeguard his personal integrity, especially if the subject is in a dependent relationship to the investigator.

4b. At any time during the course of clinical research the subject or his guardian should be free to withdraw permission for research to be continued. The investigator or the investigating team should discontinue the research if in his or their judgment it may, if continued, be harmful to the individual.

Ethical Guidelines for Clinical Investigation, 1966
American Medical Association—Opinion of the Judicial Council

The following guidelines are intended to aid physicians in fulfilling their ethical responsibilities when they engage in the clinical investigation of new drugs and procedures.

1. A physician may participate in clinical investigation only to the extent that his activities are a part of a systematic program competently designed, under accepted standards of scientific research, to produce data which is scientifically valid and significant.
2. In conducting clinical investigation, the investigator should demonstrate the same concern and caution for the welfare, safety and comfort of the person involved as is required of a physician who is furnishing medical care to a patient independent of any clinical investigation.
3. In clinical investigation *primarily for treatment*
   A. The physician must recognize that the physician-patient relationship exists and that he is expected to exercise his professional judgment and skill in the best interest of the patient.
   B. Voluntary consent must be obtained from the patient, or from his legally authorized representative if the patient lacks the capacity to consent, following: (a) disclosure that the

physician intends to use an investigational drug or experimental procedure, (b) a reasonable explanation of the nature of the drug or procedure to be used, risks to be expected, and possible therapeutic benefits, (c) an offer to answer any inquiries concerning the drug or procedure, and (d) a disclosure of alternative drugs or procedures that may be available.

i. In exceptional circumstances and to the extent that disclosure of information concerning the nature of the drug or experimental procedure or risks would be expected to materially affect the health of the patient and would be detrimental to his best interests, such information may be withheld from the patient. In such circumstances such information shall be disclosed to a responsible relative or friend of the patient where possible.

ii. Ordinarily, consent should be in writing, except where the physician deems it necessary to rely upon consent in other than written form because of the physical or emotional state of the patient.

iii. Where emergency treatment is necessary and the patient is incapable of giving consent and no one is available who has authority to act on his behalf, consent is assumed.

4. In clinical investigation *primarily for the accumulation of scientific knowledge*

A. Adequate safeguards must be provided for the welfare, safety and comfort of the subject.

B. Consent, in writing, should be obtained from the subject, or from his legally authorized representative if the subject lacks the capacity to consent, following: (a) a disclosure of the fact than an investigational drug or procedure is to be used, (b) a reasonable explanation of the nature of the procedure to be used and risks to be expected, and (c) an offer to answer any inquiries concerning the drug or procedure.

C. Minors or mentally incompetent persons may be used as subjects only if:

i. The nature of the investigation is such that mentally competent adults would not be suitable subjects.

ii. Consent, in writing, is given by a legally authorized representative of the subject under circumstances in which an informed and prudent adult would reasonably be expected to volunteer himself or his child as a subject.

D. No person may be used as a subject against his will.

Ethical Guidelines for Organ Transplantation, 1968
American Medical Association—Statement of the Judicial Council

1. In all professional relationships between a physician and his patient, the physician's primary concern must be the health of his patient. He owes the patient his primary allegiance. This concern and allegiance must be preserved in all medical procedures, including those which involve the transplantation of an organ from one person to another where both donor and recipient are patients. Care must, therefore, be taken to protect the rights of both the donor and the recipient, and no physician may assume a responsibility in organ transplantation unless the rights of both donor and recipient are equally protected.

2. A prospective organ transplant offers no justification for relaxation of the usual standards of medical care. The physician should provide his patient, who may be a prospective organ donor, with that care usually given others being treated for a similar injury or disease.

3. When a vital, single organ is to be transplanted, the death of the donor shall have been determined by at least one physician other than the recipient's physician. Death shall be determined by the clinical judgment of the physician. In making this determination, the ethical physician will use all available, currently accepted scientific tests.

4. Full discussion of the proposed procedure with the donor and the recipient or their responsible relatives or representatives is mandatory. The physician should be objective in discussing the procedure, in disclosing known risks and possible hazards, and in advising him of the alternative procedures available. The physician should not encourage expectations beyond those which the circumstances justify. The physician's interest in advancing scientific knowledge must always be secondary to his primary concern for the patient.

5. Transplant procedures of body organs should be undertaken (a) only by physicians who possess special medical knowledge and technical competence developed through special training, study, and laboratory experience and practice, and (b) in medical institutions with facilities adequate to protect the health and well-being of the parties to the procedure.

6. Transplantation of body organs should be undertaken only after careful evaluation of the availability and effectiveness of other possible therapy.

7. Medicine recognizes that organ transplants are newsworthy and that the public is entitled to be correctly informed about them. Normally, a scientific report of the procedures should first be made to the medical profession for review and evaluation. When dramatic

aspects of medical advances prevent adherence to accepted procedures, objective, factual, and discreet public reports to the communications media may be made by a properly authorized physician, but should be followed as soon as possible by full scientific reports to the profession.

In organ transplantation procedures, the right of privacy of the parties to the procedures must be respected. Without their authorization to disclose their identity the physician is limited to an impersonal discussion of the procedure.

Reporting of medical and surgical procedures should always be objective and factual. Such reporting will also preserve and enhance the stature of the medical profession and its service to mankind.

Resolution on Disapproval of Participation in Scientific Experiments by Inmates of Penal Institutions
Proceedings of the 1953 Clinical Convention of the American Medical Association, pages 91, 92, 109, and 110.

Whereas, during recent years, numerous medical and scientific experiments and research projects have been conducted partly or wholly in federal and state penal institutions; and

Whereas, volunteers among the inmates of such institutions have been permitted to participate in scientific experimental work and to submit to the administration of untested and potentially dangerous drugs; and

Whereas, some of the inmates who have so participated have not only received citations, but have in some instances been granted parole much sooner than would otherwise have occurred, including several individuals convicted of murder and sentenced to life imprisonment; and

Whereas, the Illinois State Medical Society's delegation to the American Medical Association's clinical session whole-heartedly supports research and progress in the fight against disease but does believe that persons convicted of vicious crimes should not qualify for pardon or early parole in this manner; now therefore be it

Resolved, that the House of Delegates of the American Medical Association express its disapproval of the participation in scientific experiments of persons convicted of murder, rape, arson, kidnapping, treason, or other heinous crimes, and also urges that individuals who have lost their citizenship by due process of law be considered ineligible for meritorious or commendatory citation; and be it further

Resolved, that copies of this resolution be transmitted to the Surgeons General of all federal services, the governors of all states, all officials of state and federal penal institutions and parole boards.

HOSPITAL

The Use of Investigational Drugs in Hospitals, 1952
Reprinted with permission of the American Hospital Association

This statement was prepared by the Joint Committee of the American Hospital Association and the American Society of Hospital Pharmacists to establish principles that can assist hospitals in developing procedures for the control of investigational drugs.

The document was initially approved by the AHA Board of Trustees September 28, 1957, and was also approved by the American Society of Hospital Pharmacists in 1957 and by the American Nurses' Association in 1962. The statement was reaffirmed by the AHA General Council April 12, 1973, and is hereby published to make the Association's position more widely known.

Hospitals are the primary centers for clinical investigations of new drugs. By definition, these are drugs that have not yet been released by the federal Food and Drug Administration (FDA) for general use.

Because investigational drugs have not been certified as being for general use and have not been cleared for sale in interstate commerce by the FDA, hospitals and their medical staffs have an obligation to their patients to see that proper procedures for their use are established.

Procedures for the control of investigational drugs should be based on the following principles:

- Investigational drugs should be used only under the direct supervision of the principal investigator, who should be a member of the medical staff and who should assume the burden of securing the necessary consent.
- The hospital should do all in its power to foster research consistent with adequate safeguards for its patients.
- When nurses are called upon to administer investigational drugs, they should have available to them basic information concerning such drugs—including dosage forms, strengths available, actions and uses, side effects, symptoms of toxicity, and so forth.
- The hospital should establish, preferably through the pharmacy and therapeutics committee, a central unit where essential information on investigational drugs is maintained and can be made available to authorized personnel.
- The pharmacy department is the appropriate area for storage of investigational drugs, as it is for all other drugs. This department will also provide for proper labeling and dispensing in accordance with the investigator's written orders.

APPENDIX B
SELECTED FEDERAL REGULATIONS: PROMULGATED AND PROPOSED

DEPARTMENT OF HEALTH, EDUCATION AND WELFARE

Regulations

Federal Register 40: 11854-11858 (March 13, 1975) [45 *C.F.R.*, Part 46].
"Protection of Human Subjects," effective March 13, 1975. This is a revision of the original regulations [*Federal Register* 39: 18914-18920 (May 30, 1974), effective July 1, 1974] incorporating technical amendments to conform to P.L. 93-348. The commentary published with the original regulations helps to clarify some of the language.

Federal Register 40: 22019 (May 20, 1975).
A notice permitting delay of institutional review and approval of proposals until after the proposal is submitted to DHEW.

Federal Register 40: 33526-33551 (August 8, 1975) [45 *C.F.R.*, Part 46], amended by 40: 51638 (November 6, 1975).

"Protection of Human Subjects—Fetuses, Pregnant Women, and In Vitro Fertilization," effective August 8, 1975. The Report and Recommendations of the National Commission for the Protection of Human Subjects of Biomedical and Behavioral Research is also included. The March 13, 1975, regulations were renumbered.

Proposed Rules

Federal Register 39:30648-30657 (August 23, 1974).
"Protection of Human Subjects—Fetuses, Abortuses, Pregnant Women, In Vitro Fertilization, Prisoners, and Institutionalized Mentally Infirm." The August 8, 1975, regulations cover the first four groups. The remaining two groups remain of interest.
Federal Register 40:56692-56695 (December 4, 1975).
"Protection of Identity—Research Subjects and Patients."

Draft Working Documents

Federal Register 38:31738-31749 (November 16, 1973).
"Protection of Human Subjects." Most of the groups covered by this document have been covered by more recent regulations or proposed rules. However, children as subjects have not been addressed elsewhere by DHEW.

FOOD AND DRUG ADMINISTRATION

21 Code of Federal Regulations
Part 310, "New Drugs." [§310.102 deals with consent.]
Part 312, "New Drugs for Investigational Use." [This part provides for institutional review and other controls on investigational uses of new drugs.]
Part 314, "New Drug Applications." [§314.111(a)(5) deals with study design.]
Federal Register 40:16053-16057 (April 9, 1975).
"International Research," effective May 9, 1975. This amends Part 312 to add §312.20 which sets forth the circumstances in which data generated by foreign research will be recognized by the FDA.

SELECTED
BIBLIOGRAPHY

American Psychological Association. *Ethical Principles in the Conduct of Research with Human Participants*. Washington D. C.: American Psychological Association, 1972.

Beecher, Henry K. *Research and the Individual: Human Studies*. Boston: Little, Brown and Company, 1970.

Bowers, John. "Prisoners' Rights in Prison Medical Experimentation Programs." *Clearinghouse Review*, VI, 319-333, 1972.

Bryant, Edward L., Jr. "The Burgeoning Law of Medical Experimentation Involving Human Subjects." *The John Marshall Journal of Practice and Procedure* 8 (1974): 19-51.

Capron, Alexander M. "Informed Consent in Catastrophic Disease Research and Treatment." *University of Pennsylvania Law Review* 123 (1974): 340-438.

Capron, Alexander M. "Legal Considerations Affecting Clinical Pharmacological Studies in Children." *Clinical Research* 21 (February 1973): 141-150.

Freund, Paul A., ed. *Experimentation with Human Subjects*. New York: George Braziller, 1970.

Katz, Jay (with the assistance of Alexander Capron and Eleanor Swift Glass). *Experimentation with Human Beings*. New York: Russell Sage Foundation, 1972.

Ladimer, Irving and Newman, Roger W. *Clinical Investigation in Medicine: Legal, Ethical and Moral Aspects*. Boston: Law-Medicine Research Institute, Boston University, 1963.

Ladimer, Irving, ed. "New Dimensions in Legal and Ethical Concepts for Human Research." *Annals of the New York Academy of Sciences* 169 (1970): 293-593.

Levy, C. L. *The Human Body and the Law: Legal and Ethical Considerations in Human Experimentation.* Dobbs Ferry, N. Y.: Oceana, 1975.

"Medical Treatment and Human Experimentation: Introducing Illegality, Fraud, Duress and Incapacity to the Doctrine of Informed Consent." *Rutgers-Camden Law Journal* 6 (1975): 538-564.

Merlis, Sidney, ed. *Non-scientific Constraints on Medical Research.* New York: Raven Press, 1970.

National Academy of Sciences. *Experiments and Research with Humans: Values in Conflict.* Washington D. C.: National Academy of Sciences, 1975.

"Recent Legislation Prohibiting the Use of Prison Inmates as Subjects in Medical Research." *New England Journal on Prison Law* 1 (1974): 220-243.

"Symposium: Medical Experimentation on Human Subjects." *Case Western Reserve Law Review* 25 (Spring 1975): 431-648.

U. S. Congress, Senate Committee on Labor and Public Welfare. *Quality of Health Care—Human Experimentation, 1973* (4 parts). Hearings before the Subcommittee on Health, 93rd Congress, 1st Session. Washington D. C.: U. S. Government Printing Office, 1973.

Visscher, Maurice B. *Ethical Constraints and Imperatives in Medical Research.* Springfield, Illinois: Charles C. Thomas, 1975.

Sociological Studies

Barber, Bernard; Lally, John J.; Makarushka, Julia Loughlin; and Sullivan, Daniel. *Research on Human Subjects: Problems of Social Control in Medical Experimentation.* New York: Russell Sage Foundation, 1973.

Gray, Bradford H. *Human Subjects in Medical Experimentation: A Sociological Study of the Conduct and Regulation of Clinical Research.* New York: John Wiley & Sons, 1975.

Rosenthal, Robert, and Rosnow, Ralph L. *The Volunteer Subject.* New York: John Wiley & Sons, 1975.

For a more extensive bibliography, see "Experimentation and Consent." *Bibliography of Society, Ethics and the Life Sciences.* Hastings-on-Hudson, New York: Institute of Society, Ethics and the Life Sciences, pp. 25-30, 1975.

About the Authors

Nathan Hershey is Professor of Health Law at the Graduate School of Public Health, and Research Professor of Law, School of Law, University of Pittsburgh. He has served for nearly ten years on the Graduate School of Public Health's Committee on Research Involving Human Volunteers.

In 1972 Professor Hershey served as President of the American Society of Hospital Attorneys, of which he was a board member from its inception in 1968 until 1973. He is a member of the Institute of Medicine, National Academy of Sciences and of the State Board of Medical Education and Licensure of the Commonwealth of Pennsylvania. He has also served as a consultant to various governmental bodies, including the Public Health and Welfare Committee of the Pennsylvania Senate and to private organizations.

He was an original coauthor of the Hospital Law Manual, and he has had more than 100 articles published on various health law subjects.

Professor Hershey received his undergraduate education at New York University and was graduated from the Harvard Law School in 1953.

Robert D. Miller is currently Assistant to the Director of the University of Iowa Hospitals and Clinics. He is a graduate of Iowa State University, the Yale Law School, where he served as a research assistant to Professor Jay Katz, and the Health Law Training Program at the Graduate School of Public Health, University of Pittsburgh, from which he received a Master of Science in Hygiene degree in 1975. During the 1974-1975 academic year he was a member of the Committee on Research involving Human Volunteers at the Graduate School of Public Health.